Questioning Assumptions and Challenging Perceptions

Questioning Assumptions and Challenging Perceptions

Becoming an Effective Teacher in Urban Environments

Connie L. Schaffer, Meg White,
and Corine Meredith Brown

ROWMAN & LITTLEFIELD
Lanham • Boulder • New York • London

About the cover art: The cover photo was originally a wood engraving by an unknown artist. The first known appearance of the engraving was in Camille Flammarion's 1888 book, *L'atmosphère: météorologie populaire* (*The Atmosphere: Popular Meteorology*). Subsequent renditions included the Latin words "*Urbi et Orbi*," meaning "To the City and the World."

The selection of this graphic as a cover photograph illustrates the importance of questioning assumptions and challenging perceptions. We must look beyond what we know to see the city and the world. (Licensing information: https://commons.wikimedia .org/wiki/File:Universum.jpg)

Published by Rowman & Littlefield
A wholly owned subsidiary of The Rowman & Littlefield Publishing Group, Inc.
4501 Forbes Boulevard, Suite 200, Lanham, Maryland 20706
www.rowman.com

Unit A, Whitacre Mews, 26-34 Stannary Street, London SE11 4AB

British Library Cataloguing in Publication Information Available

Library of Congress Cataloging-in-Publication Data
Names: Schaffer, Connie L., 1964– author. | White, Meg, 1961– author. |
    Brown, Corine Meredith, 1973– author.
Title: Questioning assumptions and challenging perceptions : becoming an
    effective teacher in urban environments / Connie L. Schaffer, Meg White,
    and Corine Meredith Brown.
Description: Lanham, Maryland : Rowman & Littlefield, 2016. | Includes
    bibliographical references and index.
Identifiers: LCCN 2015041376 (print) | LCCN 2015050662 (ebook) | ISBN
    9781475822021 (cloth : alk. paper) | ISBN 9781475822038 (pbk. : alk.
    paper) | ISBN 9781475822045 (electronic)
Subjects: LCSH: Education, Urban—United States. | Urban schools—United
    States. | Community and school—United States. | Teacher
    effectiveness—United States.
Classification: LCC LC5131 .S35 2016 (print) | LCC LC5131 (ebook) | DDC
    370.9173/2—dc23
LC record available at http://lccn.loc.gov/2015041376

∞™ The paper used in this publication meets the minimum requirements of American National Standard for Information Sciences—Permanence of Paper for Printed Library Materials, ANSI/NISO Z39.48-1992.

Printed in the United States of America

Contents

Foreword

Jack McKay

My assumptions guide my perceptions of how I see the world. In the classroom teaching context, my assumption is based on how I view other people, places, and events. If I come into the profession from one cultural background and I teach students in another culture, I'm faced with a variety of dilemmas, for example, differences between my background and theirs, my learning styles and theirs, and my values and theirs, to name just a few.

According to Festinger (1957) we hold many perceptions about the world and ourselves; when they clash, a discrepancy is evoked, resulting in a state of tension known as cognitive dissonance. As the experience of dissonance is unpleasant, we are motivated to reduce or eliminate it, and achieve consonance (i.e., agreement). This book provides the tools to deal with the cognitive dissonance we all cope with in teaching, leadership, and in our lives.

The authors, Schaffer, White, and Brown, have created a process to address and confront the dissonance specifically encountered by beginning teachers in classrooms of students who bring different ideas, experiences, and aspirations about themselves and their success in school.

Although the target audience of the book is teachers entering the urban school setting, the expanded targets are educators in all settings, from the rural, suburban, and urban to the professors preparing aspiring teachers and school administrators. Dissonance is not restricted to the urban school; rather it is in all educational settings. The premise of this book is based on the fact that all people, when placed in a different environment, will face the likelihood of dissonance—the difference between their cultural luggage and that of the children they teach within an urban school.

If the historical data holds, a typical beginning teacher brings a middle-class cultural background to a student population that is typically a mix of the wealthy to the poor, of the sophisticated world traveler to the youngster who has never been beyond the limits of his town or neighborhood.

The authors have successfully created a balance between the relevant theories of teaching and learning and the practice of teaching in highly complex, culturally diverse classrooms where teachers daily deal with the demands of educational technology and mandated assessments. The authors provide a beneficial, logical, and practical approach to reducing the cognitive dissonance associated with teaching to a level of understanding and approachability.

Examples of practicality are included at the end of each chapter, ranging from understanding how one thinks and sees the world:

- To being aware of the incompatibility that exists in profession;
- To the *Graffiti Wall* activity;
- To the *Sphere of Influence* that the teacher has on the students, the home, and the community;
- To the *felt need* to correct misconceptions and stereotypes about the urban school and community setting;
- To the *Culture Walk* that discovers the community's unique educational capital from which to build the foundation for educational success;
- To the *social justice* perspective that encourages action when educators encounter policies and practices that may be inequitable for the students and school.

Some examples of the significant quotes:

"The capital students bring to the classroom can serve as a conduit between their lives and the content they are studying. When teachers facilitate the connections between capital and curriculum, urban students are more than capable of meeting academic and behavioral expectations" (page 51).

"The initial Stages of Cognitive Dissonance require engagement in a process of introspection to compare what is known with what is not known. . . . creating a felt need, shifting from apprehension to appreciation, and moving beyond a deficit approach are designed to help teachers challenge their assumptions and perceptions and learn more about students" (pages 53–54).

"When teachers recognize students' assets or strengths, they can set appropriate expectations for students. . . . They do not need well-intended heroic teachers to save them from their surroundings nor do they need teachers who interact with them and their families primarily from a stance of sympathy. . . . This rescue mentality . . . implies something is wrong or deficient with urban children, their families, or their communities. As challenging as their lives may be, children living in urban communities do not have inherent deficits" (pages 48–49).

The authors have succeeded in creating a book for a much wider audience than implied in the title. This book, while targeting urban teachers, provides a solid foundation of theory and practice that should broaden the thinking of all engaged in educating the youth of our nation, from the school board member, administrator, classroom teacher, to parent advocate, in all kinds of communities. It is appropriate for educators in the rural fishing and lumber communities plagued by unemployment and alcoholism, to the suburban communities dealing with over-indulgent parenting and the abundance of recreational drugs, to the urban communities with single parent households and low-paying jobs.

Diversity and poverty are not just urban issues. These are national issues. Preparing youth to be productive citizens should be our number one priority, be it in rural or urban settings. As Horace Mann once stated, "The community school is the cornerstone of our democracy." This book is a major step toward creating an education profession that is prepared to embrace all children from all of society, and schools that are the cornerstone of our nation's success.

—Jack McKay, EdD, executive director
of the Horace Mann League of the USA

Acknowledgments

We wish to acknowledge:

The power and privilege of living in a society that embraces collaborative technology. Although open access to tools such as Web-based document sharing, video conferencing, and social media is often taken for granted, this was essential to our professional partnership and the completion of this book.

Kappa Delta Pi and the Association of Teacher Educators for connecting us with each other and for providing the professional networking opportunities which transformed this book from a notion, to a concept, to a plan, and finally to a reality.

The University of Nebraska at Omaha, Stockton University, and Rowan University for pushing us to engage in research and supporting us with the necessary resources to accomplish our goals.

Our peer readers, Linda Brown-Bartlett, Sarah Edwards, and Lela Nix, for their constructive critique of our writing as well as other colleagues for their input and insights on urban education and constant confidence in our abilities. Perhaps more importantly we recognize the uncanny ability of our colleagues to know which of these we needed at any given moment—even when we did not.

The distinguished scholars Sonia Nieto, H. Richard Milner IV, and Jack McKay, for taking time to help us as first-time authors and for their enthusiastic endorsements of our work.

The publishing team at Rowman & Littlefield, especially Sarah Jubar. Sarah, thank you for the cup of coffee in Phoenix, for representing our voices to the editorial team at Rowman & Littlefield, for your quick and thorough responses to our many questions, and for believing in us.

The inspiration we receive from urban students and teachers. Our work is motivated by your talent, intellect, and the incredible possibilities you represent.

—Connie Schaffer
—Meg White
—Cori Brown

Introduction

"Your assumptions are your windows on the world. Scrub them off every once in a while or the light won't come in. If you challenge your own, you won't be so quick to accept the unchallenged assumptions of others."

— Alan Alda[1]

An assumption is a belief individuals accept as truth and often take for granted as fact. A perception is the vantage point from which individuals view people, places, and things; it is how a person contemplates the world. Individuals, including teachers, make many assumptions and have numerous preconceived notions, some of which pertain to people who are different than they are and environments unfamiliar to them. These assumptions influence people's perceptions.

Because urban environments include some of the nation's most heterogeneous populations, individuals who teach in urban schools will have classrooms filled with students who are different from them and who come from varied backgrounds. Depending on the cultural background of a specific teacher, these differences can be represented in the race, ethnicity, language, religion, family structure, and/or socioeconomic status of the students. Teachers may make assumptions or have perceptions of urban students based on these differences.

These preconceptions often exist at a subconscious level and are likely to go unnoticed. As the opening quote suggests, it is important for teachers to *scrub them off every once in a while* in order to incorporate new information and perspectives into existing beliefs and viewpoints. Considering the hectic nature of daily life and the complex demands of preparing for today's classrooms, many teachers have limited opportunities to examine their existing assumptions.

While the preponderance of literature describes how teachers should teach students in urban settings, this book asserts that individuals cannot be effective teachers in urban schools without first understanding their assumptions and perceptions of urban schools and the students who attend them. What exists on a subconscious level must be brought into the conscious awareness of teachers and exposed to *the light* of additional external information.

The Theory of Cognitive Dissonance, described in depth in chapter 1, is referenced throughout this book (Festinger, 1957). Using the Theory of Cognitive Dissonance, readers will have multiple opportunities to *scrub off* their assumptions. They will consider what they know as they examine their personal beliefs and perceptions. They will also consider what they do not know as they investigate new information and varied perspectives.

As readers progress through subsequent chapters, they will realize *they don't know what they don't know.* This book guides readers through the process of questioning their assumptions and challenging their perceptions of urban communities, urban schools, and urban students.

Chapters 1 through 6 contain sections entitled Understanding the Concept. In these sections information to deepen the understanding of educational theory and concepts provides the background readers will need to formulate answers to the Essential Questions that frame the chapters. These Essential Questions include:

- How does the exploration of personal beliefs, actions, and experiences allow for better understanding the lives of others?
- What are common perceptions of urban environments?
- How does the social context of living in urban environments affect students prior to entering the classroom?
- In what ways is cognitive dissonance created in teachers whose background is different from their students?
- How can cognitive dissonance created within an individual begin to impact society?
- How can personal knowledge transform into professional action?

   Chapters 1 through 6 also contain Making it Personal sections, which include experiential learning activities. As readers progress through each chapter, the Making it Personal sections engage the reader with the text through experiential learning activities. Through these interactive, introspective, and reflective activities related to the central concepts, the learning process is personalized to individual readers. The activities are written in a conversational tone to establish a personal dialogue with individual readers.

   While readers will spend considerable time reflecting on their internally held assumptions and perceptions, chapters 5 and 6 present ways to act in the external spheres of their classrooms, schools, communities, and the profession. The concept of social justice is a central focus of these chapters. The final chapter provides a powerful case study depicting the central concepts addressed in the book.

   When readers turn the final page of this book, they will not be finished questioning their assumptions and challenging their perceptions. They will have gained knowledge and experiences, allowing them to continue this process and be on their way to becoming effective teachers in urban environments.

NOTE

   1. Alda, A. (1980). "62nd Commencement Address" (1980). Commencement Addresses, Paper 7. Alda's quote was taken from a commencement address given at Connecticut College. The quote has also been attributed to Isaac Asimov.

1

Personal Exploration

Essential Question: *How does the exploration of personal beliefs, actions, and experiences allow for better understanding the lives of others?*

Experiential Learning: *To understand others requires an understanding of oneself.*

Consider the expression *people don't know what they don't know.* If people are raised in a middle-class or working-class family, what they know is shaped, in part, by the people in their lives. Perhaps their parents worked or were divorced; maybe some were raised by grandparents. Many families relocate and children change schools. People come from varying cultural backgrounds and differing socioeconomic groups, and for the most part, that is what they know.

Through life experiences of what is seen, what is learned from home, and how people view themselves and others, stereotypes develop. Stereotypes can be created from media-based perceptions, or from what is learned from friends, family members, and colleagues, but *people don't know what they don't know.* For example, if they have never experienced an urban setting or an urban school, they cannot adequately compare it to what they think they know.

A critical component of effective teaching involves examining students' lives and the various stereotypes students encounter. An effective urban educator must come to understand all children in nonstereotypical ways by "acknowledging and comprehending the ways in which culture and content influence their lives and learning" (Darling-Hammond, 2002, p. 209).

The consideration of personal beliefs and cultural identity must precede pedagogy. Ladson-Billings (2011) suggests that the initial consideration should be how to think, rather than "what to do" or how to teach (p. 34). Specifically, teachers should not only address how they think about curriculum and instruction, but also how they think about social context and their students.

In order to be effective in any learning environment, teachers should consider "attitudes and beliefs about their students, their relationships with them, and their knowledge about their families and backgrounds" (Nieto, 2013, p. 20). This careful examination helps teachers formulate an initial set of beliefs and perceptions about the cultural identity of students. Cultural identity can include, but is not limited to, race, ethnicity, language, customs, family roles, and religious beliefs.

Assumptions are often made about cultural identity. The cultural identity of some students will be quite familiar and comfortable to teachers, as certain physical characteristics, languages, and family customs may be similar to what was present in one's own childhood and young adulthood. The cultural identity of other students will be quite different, and perhaps less comfortable and lacking similarity to one's own experiences.

For example, if certain physical characteristics, spoken languages, and/or family customs are unknown, possibly even misunderstood, the cultural stereotypes created about these students are likely to be less positive. Cultural factors such as language, customs, family roles, and religious beliefs contribute not only to the overall life experiences of each person, but specific experiences in the classroom as well. Teachers need to "recognize the important influence culture has on learning" (Gay, 2010, p. 45). Before teachers consider the cultural identity of students, it is important for them to consider their own cultural identity.

MAKING IT PERSONAL: HOW DO
YOU DEFINE YOUR CULTURAL IDENTITY?

In this experiential learning activity, think about what you know about yourself as you begin the process of personal discovery and exploration. There are two parts to this activity. In the first part, you are going to consider your own cultural identity and how you define yourself. Answer the following questions in your response, as you engage in thoughtful introspection:

- What is your ethnic background, religious affiliation, native language, gender identity, and socioeconomic class? What other information might you include in the description of your cultural identity?
- Would others who do not know you well describe you differently? If so, how?
- What stereotypes exist in those descriptions?

For the second part of the activity, choose someone from the array of photographs in Figure 1.1. Now ask the same questions from the first part of

**Figure 1.1.
Photographs of Students**

the activity and attempt to answer them as you would if you were *this person* in the photograph you selected. When you have finished writing your responses to the questions, share your results. Be ready to discuss your impressions and how you arrived at these impressions. What stereotypes might you have about this person's cultural identity based solely on appearance?

These activities are meant not only to elicit a response to how you self-identify, but also to demonstrate how quickly you make assumptions about people you may not know very well. This awareness about cultural identities is an important initial step to understanding yourself and your students.

UNDERSTANDING THE CONCEPT: ESTABLISHING A FRAME OF REFERENCE

Through discussion and activities, this book provides a platform to question ingrained knowledge and assumptions and understand how these fit into the context of teaching and learning in an urban setting. A person's existing knowledge and perceptions form their frame of reference.

What are the implications of a teacher's frame of reference? For teachers, knowing who they are individually, understanding the contexts of where they teach, and "questioning their knowledge and assumptions are as important as the mastery of techniques for instructional effectiveness" (Gay & Kirkland, 2003, p. 181).

Teachers may begin to realize how personal experience alone may create limited perceptions, as there is a world beyond what is currently known to them. They must consider what may have been "emphasized and omitted" in their own education and in what ways their "lived experiences growing up" contribute to their worldview (Schultz, 2008, p. 145). Cognitive dissonance may be a means for teachers to challenge their existing worldviews.

According to Leon Festinger (1957), cognitive dissonance is created when people try to hold incompatible ideas (cognitions) simultaneously. These conflicting beliefs often bring discomfort and uncertainty (dissonance). For example, someone smokes or knows someone who enjoys smoking (1st cognition). However, this person knows it is an unhealthy habit (2nd cognition). A smoker's thoughts begin to conflict (dissonance) with what he or she knows, which is that smoking is both enjoyable and unhealthy.

Another example of cognitive dissonance can be found in Aesop's fable about the fox and the grapes:

> One hot summer's day a fox was strolling through an orchard till he came to a bunch of grapes just ripening on a vine which had been trained over a lofty branch. "Just the thing to quench my thirst," quoth he. Drawing back a few paces, he took a run and a jump, and just missed the bunch. Turning round again with a One, Two, Three, he jumped up, but with no greater success. Again and again he tried after the tempting morsel, but at last had to give it up, and walked away with his nose in the air, saying: "I am sure they are sour" ("The fox and the grapes").

In the case of the fox, his initial thought or cognition upon seeing the grapes was that he could readily quench his thirst. His experience of repeatedly jumping to reach the grapes led to a different cognition—his thirst would not be quenched as easily as he originally thought it would. As he attempted to resolve his original cognition with the new information he gained through his experiences, he was faced with uncertainty or dissonance. This ultimately led him to give up and walk away.

To see an example of cognitive dissonance within the field of education, consider the vast majority of teachers around the country who are predominantly female, white, middle class, and teach in classrooms different from the ones they attended as students. What they know from their own upbringing (1st cognition) is different from what they might be seeing in an urban classroom (2nd cognition). How can female, white, middle-class teachers be successful in an urban classroom if what they know about urban schools and classrooms is incompatible (dissonance) with what they know about or how they were taught in suburban or rural schools and classrooms?

Festinger (1957) suggests three ways to resolve this dissonance; people can: 1) change their beliefs, 2) change their actions, or 3) change perceptions of their actions. Using the previous examples, the fox declared the grapes to be sour, which was a change in his belief. A smoker may decide to quit, which would be a change of action. And finally, a smoker may also declare *I am going to die one day anyway, so what is the difference?*

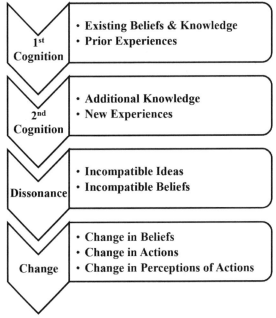

Figure 1.2.   Cognitive Dissonance

This is a change in the perception of an action. Figure 1.2 illustrates Festinger's Theory of Cognitive Dissonance.

Teachers must understand what they experience teaching in an urban classroom may be different than what they experienced as elementary and secondary students. As a result, they begin to either change beliefs or actions in order to work through the dissonance.

Noted author and leading advocate for children who attend urban schools Lisa Delpit explains that the success of urban teachers is contingent upon a greater understanding of their students. "Their success is not because their skin color matches their students, but because they know the *lives* and *culture* of their students. Knowing students is a prerequisite for teaching them well" (Delpit, 2012, p. 87). In other words, teachers do not need to be of the same color, racial background, or ethnicity as their students to effectively teach them.

To embrace cognitive dissonance is first to embrace the notion of the unknown. Simply put, people do not know everything. When individuals encounter new ideas or new bodies of knowledge, this new information conflicts or contradicts with past experiences, how they think, or what they believe they already know.

Cognitive dissonance can help people to understand cultural identity. Culture is a complex term that carries unique meaning to individuals. The influences of social institutions (family, religion, education, and government) impact personal beliefs, values, traditions, and experiences. In addition, race, ethnicity, sexual orientation, socioeconomic status, and language all contribute to a personal cultural background.

MAKING IT PERSONAL: ABCs OF CULTURAL UNDERSTANDING AND COMMUNICATION

The following experiential learning activity is a personal exploration of your cultural identity, including family traditions, religious beliefs, and community life. Revealing experiences and issues throughout childhood and early adulthood relating to ethnicity, race, gender, and ability allows you to better understand and explain who you are and how you live. This then gives you the capacity to begin to engage in conversation with others about their lives. This activity consists of three parts: *A*utobiography, *B*iography, and *C*ross-cultural analysis (adapted from Schmidt & Finkbeiner, 2006).

A: Autobiography

As previously discussed, before you begin to understand others, you need to understand yourself and how this may influence your relationships with others. In this activity you will narrate, analyze, and reflect on deep-rooted cultural features of your background. Think of this activity as having three parts: narrative, analysis, and reflection.

First, *narrate* the experiences you consider of significance in shaping your worldview. How do you self-identify your own ethnic/cultural background? You may include typical and/or exceptional events from your childhood, school years, religious life, family life, as well as memorable encounters with individuals of varied backgrounds.

You may also want to think about how your race, ethnicity, language, class, family background, religious beliefs, and gender may have shaped your life thus far. Rather than providing a lengthy list of experiences and elements of your identity, choose those most significant to you, or most relevant to your future as an educator.

Consider the following questions as you write. These questions serve as a guide, not a script, to your writing.

- In what ways has your family influenced your own self-identity?
- What experiences within your immediate or extended families allowed the exploration of your worldview?
- How do the people in the neighborhood where you live (or lived) exemplify differences in socioeconomic status, racial diversity, or other aspects of diversity?
- To what extent did you experience anyone who was different from you while you were in school or growing up?
- How does your ability or disability impact your experiences in school or in other contexts?
- How were gender roles defined for you in your upbringing or during a certain life experience (i.e., sports or extracurricular activities)? Were there different expectations for gender roles in your family or in other contexts?
- How has your native language impacted your cultural identity?
- How did/does your native language impact your academic experiences or interactions with native English speakers?
- What experiences have you had with racism or other forms of discrimination in your life in school, your family, or other contexts?
- What experiences have you had in life or in school that may have contributed to an underlying perception there is something wrong or insufficient with other cultures, races, genders, and/or religions different from your own?
- Are there specific experiences in your upbringing or education that promoted a white, middle-class culture?

Second, consider how these events and experiences have shaped your worldview and *analyze* how this has played a role in the development of your:

- *thinking* (your personal thoughts),
- *behavior* (your personal actions and physical responses to these events), and

- *perceptions* (your judgment and decision of what is important about an event or experience).

What do these experiences mean? Finally, *reflect* on what you have learned about yourself while writing the cultural autobiography. What has this process helped you to discover about your identity and your future as a teacher? As you reflect, you might consider the following questions:

- How do your values influence your attitudes toward children?
- How do you think about differences in children, and do you implicitly equate difference with deficiency?
- Do you think all children can learn?
- How will writing this autobiography impact your work as an educator?

B: Biography

The biography components of the *ABC* activity allow you to construct meaning and develop a deeper understanding of another person's life. Using the framework from the cultural autobiography, interview someone who is culturally different from you. For example, if you are white, you may choose to interview a person of color. If you grew up in a large city in the United States, you may want to interview someone who was raised in a rural area or perhaps spent a significant part of their childhood in another country.

With the information you collected, write a biography of this person. Attempt to parallel the content of this biography to your autobiography by asking this person similar questions to those you answered for yourself.

C: Cross-Cultural Analysis

For the final part of the *ABC* activity, conduct a cross-cultural analysis by creating a chart of differences and similarities between the autobiography and biography. Your autobiography is an example of what you know or experienced. This is your existing knowledge, referred to earlier in this chapter as the 1st cognition. The biography is an example of what you may not have known, and referred to earlier in the chapter as the 2nd cognition.

By creating a chart, you have identified the differences between the two life stories. These differences are examples of what someone else knows or has experienced that is different from your knowledge or experiences. How these experiences differ or contradict each other may lead you to reconsider what you know. This is cognitive dissonance. In the analysis of these stories, you have begun to question what you thought you knew.

CHAPTER SUMMARY

How might individuals resolve the dissonance between what they thought they knew about culture and diversity with the new information discovered throughout this chapter? Festinger (1957) suggests people can change their beliefs, actions, or perceptions of actions. For teachers, they may change or expand their beliefs regarding the unique differences represented by students in their classrooms.

This may lead teachers to change their actions and begin to interact with others in new ways. Teachers may also use alternative methods to communicate with students, parents, colleagues, or community members who are different from them. Or, teachers may engage in deeper self-reflection of their actions. They may recognize, perhaps for the first time, *that they do not know what they do not know.*

Teachers who learn about and understand their own cultural identity have greater capacity to understand and appreciate the cultural identity of their students. As a result of personal exploration and increased understanding, teachers are better prepared to effectively teach their students.

REFERENCES

Darling-Hammond, L. (2002). Educating a profession for equitable practice. In L. Darling-Hammond, J. French, & S. P. Garcia-Lopez (Eds.), *Learning to teach for social justice* (pp. 201–212). New York: Teachers College Press.

Delpit, L. (1995). *Other people's children: Cultural conflict in the classroom.* New York: The New Press.

Delpit, L. (2012). *Multiplication is for white people: Raising expectations for other people's children.* New York: The New Press.

Festinger, L. (1957). *A theory of cognitive dissonance.* Stanford: Stanford University Press.

The fox and the grapes. (1994, January 1). *Aesop's Fables*. Retrieved from www
.umass.edu/aesop/content.php?n=10&i=1

Gay, G. (2010). *Culturally responsive teaching: Theory, research, and practice*
(2nd ed.). New York: Teachers College Press.

Gay, G., & Kirkland, K. (2003). Developing cultural critical consciousness and
self-reflection in preservice teacher education. *Theory into Practice, 42*(3),
181–187.

Ladson-Billings, G. (2011). Yes, but how do we do it. In J. G. Landsman &
C. W. Lewis (Eds.), *White teachers/diverse schools: Creating inclusive
schools, building on students' diversity, and providing true educational equity*
(pp. 33–46). Sterling, VA: Stylus Publishing, LLC.

Ladson-Billings, G. (2000). Fighting for our lives: Preparing teachers to teach
African-American students. *Journal of Teacher Education, 51*(3), 206–214.

Nieto, S. (2013). *Finding joy in teaching students of diverse backgrounds: Culturally responsive and socially just practices in US classrooms*. Portsmouth,
NH: Heinemann.

Schultz, B. D. (2008). *Spectacular things happen along the way*. New York:
Teachers College Press.

Schmidt, P. R., & Finkbeiner, C. (Eds.). (2006). *ABC's of cultural understanding
and communication: National and international adaptations*. Greenwich, CT:
Information Age Publishing.

2

Creating a Definition of "Urban"

Essential Question: *What are common perceptions of urban environments?*

Experiential Learning: *It is important to understand the social context of urban environments in order to challenge perceptions of them.*

Without a doubt, differences exist between educational settings. Even within the United States, differences between school environments are quite pronounced. Each school possesses certain qualities and characteristics, creating unique distinctions between and among schools, students, and their surrounding communities. This chapter provides an opportunity to explore existing assumptions and perceptions about the context and culture of urban and other communities.

There is nothing simple about defining "urban." Just when it seems there is consensus on a particular characteristic of urban communities, schools, or students, suddenly a contradictory statement or research study appears, eliminating the certainty of the earlier pronouncement.

There are widespread perceptions urban areas present pervasive physiological needs as well as obstacles to success to the people who live there. Fewer people hold the perception urban communities contain assets helpful for children and families.

As stated in chapter 1, assumptions and perceptions of culture must be carefully examined. This holds true for school settings as well. Each school within each district exists in its own unique realm, revealing a culture and community of people specific only to this precise place. It might be similar to another school within the same district, or the differences may be quite pronounced.

For this reason, it is critical to focus attention on the socio-cultural context of individual urban schools and communities. Specifically, teachers need to consider the backgrounds of students, including "the knowledges they bring to the classroom, the languages they speak, and the ways in which all these dynamics shape learning and teaching" (Kincheloe, 2010, p. 4). An important step in doing so is to examine existing perceptions associated with urban settings.

MAKING IT PERSONAL: GRAFFITI WALL

In this experiential learning activity, you will collaborate with others to create a Graffiti Wall (Costello, 1993). You will need three large writing surfaces, such as whiteboards or large pieces of poster paper. On one, write the word *urban*. On the second, write the word *suburban*. On the third, write the word *rural*. These become the walls on which to create your graffiti.

Without providing any detail or further comments, each participant will go to the walls and write any words, phrases, and/or slang terms that come to mind when thinking about these three types of communities. These words and phrases represent your current collective perceptions of the constructs of urban, suburban, and rural. This activity frames common stereotypes of these areas and captures a collective snapshot of how these stereotypes are drawn from your backgrounds and experiences.

Your perceptions regarding the characteristics and qualities of urban, suburban, and rural settings reveal common ideas and themes among the participants, as well as unique and distinct ideas regarding these communities. A natural extension to the Graffiti Wall is for you and several of your peers to discuss similarities and differences between and among urban, suburban, and rural environments. In a group discussion, consider from where and how you arrived at your individual perceptions and/or understandings regarding the three terms.

UNDERSTANDING THE CONCEPT: SPHERE OF INFLUENCE WITHIN THE SOCIAL CONTEXT

The Graffiti Wall discussion provided opportunities to consider how people define urban environments as compared to suburban and rural. Within all environments, humans move, think, and act in relationship to others. People do not exist in a vacuum. Rather, they are constantly interacting with, influencing, and being influenced by the people and places surrounding their daily lives. This is their social context. Consider the social interactions and influences of *an individual's* immediate environment:

- What is seen, heard, smelled, and/or felt in this environment?
- Who are the people in this environment?

Social contexts will look, sound, smell, and feel different for each individual. Now, consider the social contexts of *other people,* and the individuals and places involved in *their* lives. For example, a fifth-grade girl wakes up in the morning and chats with her mother and sisters over breakfast before school. She then gets on a bus to go to school, where she laughs and jokes with several friends as they ride to school. These students then spend the day moving in and out of classes together.

After school dismisses, the girl goes to her father's restaurant. She helps to fold napkins and roll silverware alongside a college student working a part-time job. A couple of single mothers who work as full-time waitresses ask her about her school day. A group of elderly men, who are regulars, gather daily at the same table to drink coffee, eat cake, and play chess. As always, they invite her to join them.

This scenario describes the boundaries of the girl's social context. She lives, works, and plays within these social boundaries. She is influenced *by* these people, places, and events as she interacts with these same people, places, and events. These reciprocal interactions represent her sphere of influence.

The term "sphere of influence" originated in the field of international relations to describe a region or division of space in which a country or organization holds exclusive influence—whether through cultural, economic, military, or political might—and serves the interests of those in power outside the boundaries of that region or space. More recently, scientists in astronomy and astrodynamics, as well as analysts in data analytics, have developed ideas and uses for sphere of influence in their studies.

In the scenario above and throughout this book, the sphere of influence is modified for educational purposes. A sphere of influence is defined as the psychological, social, and physical perimeters in which a person influences others and/or is influenced by others (Levine, 1972). The sphere of influence in the above application focused on three entities: the home, the school, and the community.

A sphere of influence may initially develop on a small scale in the innermost core. People are born into specific family structures, are raised with immediate members of their group of caregivers, and come to know and understand the beliefs and values of the people in their homes.

Then the sphere broadens exponentially as people interact with school and community. Children attend preschool, elementary, middle, and high school, expanding their social context to include both home and school. Students' interactions and associations with their own community, and perhaps even communities beyond the one in which they live, further extend their social context. As students mature and seek new opportunities such as visiting the public library, getting a part-time job in the summer, or volunteering at a church or senior center, they interact with their surrounding community in new ways. This dynamic is represented in Figure 2.1.

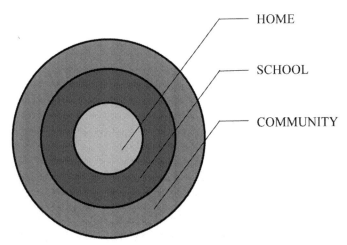

HOME

SCHOOL

COMMUNITY

Figure 2.1. Sphere of Influence within Social Context

For millions of students, their social context and sphere of influence are situated in urban areas. As such, it is necessary for teachers to understand a much broader urban context before it is possible to understand the narrowed context of a single urban student. As demonstrated in the Graffiti Wall, each individual has a current understanding or perception of "urban."

How can the Theory of Cognitive Dissonance challenge a person's *current* understanding of "urban" with new information? The process begins by examining current knowledge, then increasing the breadth and depth of existing knowledge to develop an *expanded* or *new* knowledge base.

UNDERSTANDING THE CONCEPT: DEFINITIONS OF "URBAN" BASED ON POPULATION

Providing clear definitions of "urban" leads to a more comprehensive understanding of the social contexts of urban students. Two common approaches are used to determine what environments are considered urban. One approach relies on population statistics. The other approach relies on the social characteristics used to describe the people who live in certain locations and attend specific schools. Understanding varied perspectives of what constitutes "urban" may raise awareness of current knowledge and introduce new information.

Defining urban schools may seem a simple task, but that is not the case. The manner in which urban schools are described and characterized dramatically varies. Definitions of urban schools based solely on census data of the city in which they are located are common, yet problematic. Despite the number of people who reside in a specified location, what some people perceive as urban may not be viewed as such by others.

Consider a city with a population of 500,000. It may be the largest city in the area and regionally viewed as an urban center. However, when compared to larger cities of three or four million, the first city hardly seems urban. In this case, what one person may know as "urban" is not unilaterally perceived or known as such by others.

Definitions of urban schools based only on population are problematic for another reason. Population data, even from reliable sources, are nebulous. The boundaries that define urban areas and cities are easily confused. For example, in a review of the United States Census Bureau's metropolitan statistical areas, the 2010 population of the St. Louis *metropolitan statistical area* is listed as 2,813,000 (United States Census Bureau, 2012). However, the 2010 population of the *city* of St. Louis, Missouri, in an identical search of the same source, is listed as just over 319,000. This is a difference of approximately 2.5 million people!

How is this possible? The first number is based on the multicounty area surrounding and including the independent municipality of St. Louis, Missouri, as well as numerous other smaller cities in both Missouri and Illinois. Certainly, a city with a population of over two million would be considered urban and schools within that area may be deemed urban schools. However, based on the population of the specifically defined city limits of St. Louis some people may not consider the city or its schools to be urban.

To further complicate the issue, some cities and the public school systems associated with them share the same geopolitical boundaries. Other cities have multiple public school districts within their city limits. Yet in other cases, public school districts are based on county lines even if a particular city crosses into multiple counties. These scenarios pose a conundrum; are schools considered urban based on the population of the metropolitan area, city, school district, or the county in which they are located?

This can be illustrated by comparing two similarly populated urban areas, Minneapolis, Minnesota, and San Diego, California, and their not-so-similarly sized public school districts. According to the United States Census Bureau (United States Census Bureau, 2012), the population of the Minneapolis metropolitan area (located both in Minnesota and Wisconsin) is over 3.2 million.

The largest school district in the Minneapolis metropolitan area is the Minneapolis Public Schools, which enrolls approximately 34,000 students. A number of smaller public and private schools provide education to the other children in the area. The population of San Diego is just under 3.1 million. The largest school district in this metropolitan area is the San Diego Unified School District with over 131,000 students, making its enrollment nearly three times the size of the Minneapolis Public Schools.

UNDERSTANDING THE CONCEPT:
DEFINITIONS OF "URBAN" BASED ON SOCIAL CONTEXT

If the definition of urban schools moves beyond a pure population model, then schools in a wider variety of metropolitan areas can be categorized as urban. As an alternative to using population-only statistics, other urban school definitions concentrate on the social context of an area. Ironically, both population-based and social-context definitions rely on numbers to describe urban areas.

While the number of people or students in a geographic area is the basis for population-based models, the number of students represented in a variety of socially constructed groups are the basis for social-context models. Social-context definitions frequently center on poverty levels of a school's student population. They also may rely heavily on numbers or percentages of students in groups that are defined by racial and ethnic diversity.

Social-context definitions of urban schools consider the number of students in these groups as well as the number of students with low achievement scores or the number of teachers who are considered underqualified. However, these social characteristics are not evidenced equally in all urban schools nor are they unique to schools in urban environments.

Schools in suburban and rural communities also face issues of poverty as well as other demographic characteristics used to describe urban schools. For example, the Wagner Community School District serves a rural area in South Dakota of approximately 1,500 people. This is only slightly larger than the school district's enrollment, which is approximately 1,300 students. The community of Wagner is certainly *not* recognized as urban based on population statistics.

Now consider the social context of Wagner Community Schools. First, take into account student demographics. Compared to overall demographics of South Dakota's school districts, the Wagner Community School district has a higher percentage of economically disadvantaged students. The district also has a significant enrollment of minority students. Over one-half of the student population is Native American.

In 2012–2013, the South Dakota State Report Card indicated reading and mathematics proficiency scores for Wagner Community Schools fell well below those for the state. Additionally, teachers in the district had fewer years of experience and advanced degrees than their colleagues across South Dakota (South Dakota DOE 2012–2013, Report Card). While Wagner Community Schools are *not* considered urban based only on population statistics, they *may be* considered urban based on their social context, which includes factors such as poverty, racial diversity, and educational data.

UNDERSTANDING THE CONCEPT: BROADENING THE DEFINITION OF "URBAN"

Just as population-based definitions are inadequate, definitions that rely only on educational and/or achievement variables are also problematic as they are likely to contribute to a single story of urban schools and perpetuate the stereotype that urban schools have inherent educational deficits. Furthermore, focusing only on these elements to define urban schools minimizes the immense bureaucratic scope of providing education to children in cities with a large population base and districts with high student enrollments.

Milner (2012) suggests a method to classify urban school districts. His model is based primarily on population but also considers the context of the surrounding community by recognizing social, economic, and academic factors impacting schools. Milner's approach creates a three-tiered categorization of urban districts, thus expanding the definition of urban schools to incorporate multiple perspectives of what constitutes an urban school and broadening the discussion to include educators in a variety of locations.

Based on Milner's typology, which classifies urban school districts as either urban intensive, urban emergent, or urban characteristic, Figure 2.2 illustrates the variation of what might be considered urban. The first two categories are clearly urban, based both on population and socioeconomic variables. Urban intensive schools are those in major metropolitan areas with over one million residents.

Schools in the largest urban areas such as New York, New York; Chicago, Illinois; and Los Angeles, California are quickly identified. This category includes a number of other large cities such as Baltimore, Maryland; Jacksonville, Florida; Minneapolis, Minnesota; and Las Vegas, Nevada to name only a few.

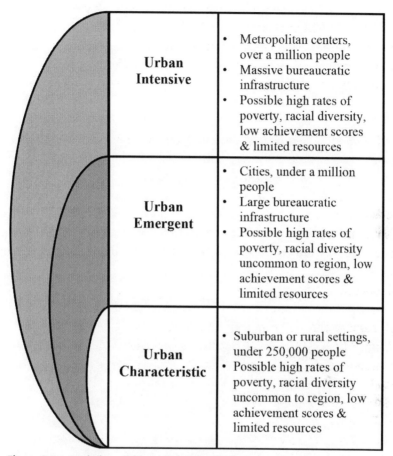

Urban Intensive	• Metropolitan centers, over a million people • Massive bureaucratic infrastructure • Possible high rates of poverty, racial diversity, low achievement scores & limited resources
Urban Emergent	• Cities, under a million people • Large bureaucratic infrastructure • Possible high rates of poverty, racial diversity uncommon to region, low achievement scores & limited resources
Urban Characteristic	• Suburban or rural settings, under 250,000 people • Possible high rates of poverty, racial diversity uncommon to region, low achievement scores & limited resources

Figure 2.2. Variation within Urban School Districts

Urban emergent schools are situated in metropolitan areas with large populations, but fewer than one million residents. While it may be more difficult to think of these examples, school districts in El Paso, Texas; Omaha, Nebraska; Akron, Ohio; and Fresno, California would be classified as urban emergent.

The third category, urban characteristic districts, includes schools that are not located in large population centers but may share the socioeconomic profiles and educational challenges similar to schools in the other two categories. They also share many other social context variables found in urban emergent and urban intensive school districts. The rural school in South Dakota referred to earlier has characteristics often associated with urban schools (poverty, racial diversity, and low test scores), but clearly is not located within a metropolitan setting.

Using the population base of metropolitan statistical areas and social context variables often associated with urban schools, Fgure 2.3 provides a geographic snapshot of several cities and towns along with their corresponding populations. The size and scope of the urban school districts located within these areas are summarized in Table 2.1.

It is important to note that, even within these districts, the social context of individual schools may vary considerably, including the racial, ethnic, socioeconomic, and educational characteristics of their students and teachers.

Identifying urban schools is not a simple undertaking. Definitions of urban schools focused on *either* a population perspective *or* a social context perspective are inadequate and portray an incomplete picture of urban

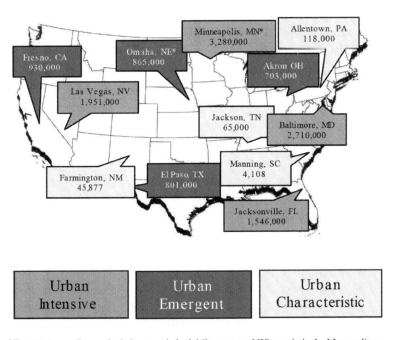

*The US Census Bureau includes areas in both Minnesota and Wisconsin in the Metropolitan Statistical Area of Minneapolis, and areas in both Nebraska and Iowa for the Metropolitan Statistical Area of Omaha. City Populations - Metropolitan statistical area as reported in U.S. Census Bureau, Statistical Abstract of the United States: 2012 census.gov/compendia/statab/&census.gov/popfinder/https://census.gov/popfinder/

Figure 2.3. Populations of Urban School Districts—A Cross Section of the United States

Table 2.1.   Size and Scope of Urban Districts

Location	Largest School District	Student Population	Number of Full–Time Teachers	Number of School Buildings
Baltimore, MD	Baltimore City	83,800	5,736	196
Baltimore, MD	Baltimore County	104,160	7,455	173
Jacksonville, FL	Duval	123,997	7,993	191
Minneapolis, MN	Minneapolis	34,934	2,394	98
Las Vegas, NV	Clark County	314,059	15,269	377
Akron, OH	Akron City	23,113	1,709	56
Omaha, NE	Omaha	49,405	3,369	98
El Paso, TX	El Paso	64,330	4,399	107
Fresno, CA	Fresno	74,883	3,093	106
Allentown, PA	Allentown City	17,637	1,218	23
Manning, SC	Clarendon 02	3,047	151	6

Both Baltimore City and Baltimore County Public Schools are large school districts within the Baltimore Metropolitan Statistical Area. Although Baltimore City is the smaller of the two, based on its location and the population density patterns within Baltimore, the National Center of Education Statistics classifies it as a "city" school and Baltimore County as a "suburban" school. To create a comprehensive representation of the Baltimore area, both districts are included in this table.

Sources: School district data, National Center for Education Statistics (2010–2011) http://nces.ed.gov/ccd/districtsearch/; http://nces.ed.gov/ccd/districtsearch/

schools. If teachers are to become effective urban educators, they must examine factors beyond population and enrollment statistics to develop an understanding of the social context in which their students live and learn.

MAKING IT PERSONAL: MOVING BEYOND A SINGLE STORY OF URBAN SCHOOLS

This two-part experiential learning activity illustrates the varied contexts of urban schools. Using two school districts referenced in Figure 2.3 or by selecting two urban emergent or intensive districts of interest to you, create a statistical profile for each district.

Part One: No Two Urban Districts Are the Same

For each district, research the most recent data related to the following:

- Total student population
- Racial and ethnic demographics of the student population
- Number or percentage of students who receive free or reduced meals

- Number or percentage of students in programs for English-language learners
- Number or percentage of students with Individual Education Plans
- Mobility rates for students
- High school graduation rates
- Number or percentage of students who meet or exceed state testing requirements
- Number or percentage of teachers who meet certification requirements
- Average years of experience for teachers
- Number or percentage of teachers with advanced degrees

Do not expect to find the statistics concisely presented in one source. Research multiple reliable sources. You may want to begin your research with the Department of Education website for the state in which the districts are located as well as the school districts' websites. Other valuable sources include the National Center for Education Statistics and the Kids Count Data Center.

Using the information you find, create an infographic representation of both districts. Infographics are depictions of complex data or information in a concise and visually appealing manner. Consider using a combination of graphic organizers, pie charts, bar graphs, or other images to visually depict the similarities and differences of the two urban districts.

Part Two: No Two Urban Schools Are the Same

Even within the same school district, individual buildings and their surrounding communities can dramatically vary. Repeat the activity in part one, but select two or more school buildings within the same urban school district. Create a second infographic depiction of the similarities and differences between the schools.

From the information gathered in this activity, your definition of what constitutes urban is likely expanding to include cities, towns, school districts, and even individual schools that perhaps you did not previously associate with urban environments. Researching on your own, compiling informational statistics, and creating an infographic synthesizes what "urban" looks like in the United States today.

CHAPTER SUMMARY

There is not a single story or context of any district or school. Considering more detailed definitions of urban districts and urban schools allows teachers to strengthen their conceptual framework through cognitive dissonance. This chapter has presented expanded definitions of "urban" to include urban intensive, urban emergent, and urban characteristic. With this broadened definition, it is likely a person's initial understanding of what defines urban districts (1st cognition) changes based on new information (2nd cognition). Dissonance is created when people begin to question what constitutes urban. This supports the idea *people don't know what they don't know.*

In short summary, context matters. The social contexts of urban intensive, emergent, and characteristic schools have a tremendous influence on children, families, and educators. When educators understand the social context of urban schools, it creates a foundation for recognizing the unique needs of urban students. Teachers must recognize the impact of racial and linguistic diversity, socioeconomic factors, and educational infrastructures across the nation and within single localities.

Individual actions of each teacher will be shaped by an understanding of the social context in which he or she teaches. When teachers' understanding of the broader context of urban schools is enhanced, they can begin to see how social context impacts individual students. Further discussion of social context is addressed in chapter 3.

REFERENCES

Costello, C. (1993). Graffiti—A positive approach. *Notes Plus*, October, 6–7.

Kids Count Data Center. (2014). Retrieved from: www.datacenter.kidscount.org/

Kincheloe, J. L. (2010). Why a book on urban education? In S. R. Steinberg (Ed.), *19 urban questions: Teaching in the city* (pp. 1–26). New York: Peter Lang Publishing, Inc.

Levine, J. H. (1972). The sphere of influence. *American Sociological Review, 37*(1), 14–27. Retrieved from www.dartmouth.edu/~jlevine/Sphere%20of%20 Influence%20Levine.pdf

Milner, H. R. (2012). But what is urban education? *Urban Education, 47*(3), 556–561.

National Center for Education Statistics. (2010–2011). Retrieved from: www
.nces.ed.gov/ccd/districtsearch/

South Dakota DOE 2012–2013, Report Card (2013). Retrieved from: www.doe
.sd.gov/reportcard/

U.S. Census Bureau. (2012). City populations—Metropolitan statistical areas as
reported in *Statistical Abstract of the United States*, Washington, DC: Author.

3

The Social Context of Children and Families in Urban Environments

Essential Question: *How does the social context of living in urban environments affect students prior to entering the classroom?*

Experiential Learning: *To understand others, there must be an understanding of the places they live.*

This chapter addresses the issue of how social context affects children. It is essential for teachers to understand this context in order to better teach students. Too often, teachers "conform to 'best practices' and miss the opportunity to actually get to know and reach their students" (Schultz, 2008, p. 146). Understanding the social context of urban students is an important step in getting to know them.

Chapter 2 established the broad social context of what is considered urban. It is also necessary to increase the depth of knowledge regarding specific factors of social context, which impact individuals. While great variety exists in urban settings, the stark reality is that many urban children attend schools in areas marked by profound economic hardship.

More than 80 percent of high-density poverty areas in the United States are located in the nation's one hundred largest cities (Kincheloe, 2010). A serious lack of resources exists within the physical boundaries of poverty—including but not limited to healthy food options, green spaces to play, and digital access.

Living in poverty can directly affect a child's ability to actively participate and fully engage in areas of life beyond meeting the most basic needs.
While the impact of poverty is manifested in many ways, children who
come from a low socioeconomic background may struggle with attendance
in school, academic performance, and overall health and wellness.

Consider the story of Amie that will be outlined below in Case Study
3.1. Amie grew up poor. While not all children who come from low-
income families face the challenges Amie did, her story exemplifies the
impact social context can have on the physical, psychological, and educational development of children.

CASE STUDY 3.1: THE STORY OF AMIE (PSEUDONYM)

Meet Amie. She is somewhat reserved, but has a contagious smile and
sparkling eyes. She is artistically talented, devoted to her family, loyal to
her friends, and has tremendous perseverance. She grew up in the largest
city in her midwestern state. She attended the largest high school within
the largest school district in this state. Growing up, she was an urban student, and she was poor.

When I got holes in the bottoms of my shoes, my friend's parents made sure
I got different shoes. My parents couldn't get me shoes or much of anything.
My father was in and out of prison and never really in my life. My mother
battled mental illness and was not capable of raising me and my siblings. I
took care of myself, my younger brother and sister, and my mother because
she was not able to care for us. I used to go to bed hungry. I remember
stealing a sandwich from school. The security guard caught me. I knew I
was in trouble, but the security guard knew me well. He was the one who
often found me walking the streets and would take me to school. He did not
make a big deal about the sandwich. I was lucky.

Dealing with the challenges she faced at home left Amie with little
capacity for school-related tasks.

Some days I could not be engaged in school because the night before had
just been too bad. I just wanted to lay my head on the desk because I was
exhausted, and I was embarrassed. It wasn't that I was choosing not to
focus, I could not focus—literally. I knew teachers were frustrated with me.

Heck, I was frustrated with them telling me what to do. I didn't know how to respond to someone telling me what to do because I was usually the one telling the people in my life what to do.

Exasperated, Amie frequently used vulgar language in the classroom and refused to do her schoolwork. Her attendance record was abysmal.

I knew I was difficult. The teachers thought I did not know how they felt about me. But I heard their comments and read their body language. I knew some of them would rather I be absent than have me in class. I missed a lot of school. Not once did a teacher ask me why I was absent. I wonder now if that would have made a difference.

There were teachers who acknowledged me and helped me feel included. Several teachers noticed my potential and treated me as "not lesser than" the other students. There was one art teacher who always noticed when I was at school and would find ways to compliment me—even if it was for something simple like being on time. I purposefully failed that class because I wanted to be there.

By age seventeen, Amie had passed only two high school courses.

I couldn't wait to get out of school so I could find a job and take care of my brother and sister. I dropped out at age eighteen and was spending my time out in the streets, not caring about education. I was a ward of the state so I had a caseworker. He encouraged me to take a GED class. I enrolled, and within two weeks I passed the test. For the first time in my life I realized I was smart.

After passing my GED, I started to gain confidence. Maybe I could go to college. My caseworker and juvenile court judge saw something in me and kept encouraging me. I had always tuned out the conversations about college because we had no money. But in reality, no one ever asked me if I wanted to go to college.

Today, Amie continues to live in the same city. As a result of her determination, she did attend college and studied to be a teacher (Amie, personal communication, December 10, 2014).

Throughout her childhood, Amie struggled to meet the very basic necessities of life. Physically, she experienced hunger. She did not have appropriate clothing nor did she get adequate sleep. Psychologically, she lacked the sense of safety and security most children get from their parents or caregivers. She put herself in dangerous situations when she was on the streets. Due to a constant struggle to meet basic physical and psychological needs, Amie had little motivation for school in her early life.

UNDERSTANDING THE CONCEPT:
MASLOW'S IDENTIFICATION OF HUMAN NEEDS

Psychologist Abraham Maslow (1943) spent much of his career studying what drives humans to succeed. He believed each person is motivated to fulfill certain needs. Primary to Maslow's theory was the premise: as lower needs are satisfied, people strive to acquire and/or achieve the next need level, ultimately working toward the highest level on a pyramid of needs.

Contemporary interpretations of Maslow's work present the needs as categories that are not hierarchical in relationship to one another. In these interpretations, it is important to note people will move in and between these stages throughout their lives. Fluctuation is natural and expected. The inability to meet needs at a lower level does not prevent meeting needs at a higher level. Table 3.1 shows categories of needs represented in Maslow's original hierarchy (Maslow, 1943).

People may find it difficult to address the various needs without meeting those Maslow placed at lower levels. Food, shelter, and clothing are the three most basic needs of survival. For children growing up in poverty, it is difficult to come to school hungry and think about much more than just being hungry. This may impede their ability to form relationships with their peers and to develop confidence to sustain academic achievement. Subsequently, this may impair their ability to satisfy the need for self-actualization, wherein they engage in creative problem solving.

Yet there are also incredible examples of people who have lived without access to consistent food, safe shelter, and clothing who defy expectations and exceed beyond their circumstances. Consider children who lived through the Great Depression in the 1930s, child refugees from Rwanda and other countries who experience violence and loss of homes, and the unspeakable horrors faced by Jewish children and adult survivors in Nazi concentration camps. There is a power of individual human spirit, deter-

Table 3.1. Maslow's Hierarchy of Needs

Self-actualization	morality, creativity, problem-solving
Self-esteem	confidence, achievement, respect
Love & belonging	friendship, family
Safety	security, family, health, property
Physiological	breathing, food, water

mination, and perseverance beyond measure by any one approach to achievement on a hierarchy, table, or chart.

While not all children living in urban areas experience the effects of poverty, it is a factor for a significant number of children attending urban schools. Poverty rates are not only high in urban areas; poverty is often highly concentrated within urban neighborhoods. These are areas where poverty rates meet or exceed 30 percent (Nichols, 2013).

In 2014, 14 percent of children in the United States lived in areas of concentrated poverty (Kids Count, 2014). Concentrated poverty exacerbates the already significant challenges of living in poverty. "Living in areas with many other poor people places burdens on low-income families beyond what the families' own individual circumstances would dictate . . . and results in higher crime rates, underperforming public schools, poor housing and health conditions, as well as limited access to private services and job opportunities" (Bishaw, 2011, p. 1). Table 3.2 illustrates the needs originally outlined in Maslow's Hierarchy and how they apply to children in poverty.

Table 3.2. Challenges Faced by Children Who Live in Poverty

Self-actualization	• Individuals may find it difficult to fulfill their potential. • Education may not be seen as a viable means of attaining goals.
Self-esteem	• Confidence and motivation to maintain sustained achievement in school and other settings may be lacking. • Respect for academic achievement may be minimized.
Love & belonging	• Ability to build long-term, positive relationships with peers may be compromised. • Emotional connections with adults, including teachers may be difficult.
Safety	• Homes may be overcrowded and located in high-crime neighborhoods. • Feelings of safety, security, and dependence on adults may be inconsistent.
Physiological	• Life-sustaining needs such as food, shelter, and clothing may not be guaranteed. • Access to healthcare may be sporadic or nonexistent.

Table 3.2 outlines challenges that may be faced by children who live in poverty as they relate to Maslow's Hierarchy of Needs (Prince & Howard, 2002). Concrete examples of these challenges are evident in the case of Amie, yet these challenges did not prevent her from achieving her goals in later life. She could not meet her basic physiological needs of food and recounts the story of stealing a sandwich from school. While she could not feel safety and dependency from her own parents, she had to provide safety and offer dependency to her siblings.

She had a difficult time connecting with most of the teachers in the school whom she felt had no understanding of what she was experiencing. With a bit of encouragement from her caseworker, Amie passed her GED exam, thus boosting her self-esteem. She realized for the first time that she was smart and college-material, though no one had asked her if she even wanted to go to college. And finally, reaching the level of self-actualization in working to complete her college degree, she reached the pinnacle of Maslow's Hierarchy.

There are many implications to children being raised in poverty and how their needs are or are not met at home or in school. Free and reduced meal statistics are commonly used to demonstrate poverty rates in schools and provide an indication of the pervasive nature of children living in poverty.

In 2012, almost 20 million children received free or reduced meals at school (U.S. Department of Agriculture, 2012). In 2014, that number jumped to over 30 million students (U.S. Department of Agriculture, 2015). As demonstrated by these statistics, there is a rapidly increasing number of children who rely on schools to meet a basic physiological need.

Before teachers consider students' academic needs, there must be an understanding of students' physical, cognitive, and psychological needs. Poverty impacts each of these needs. Gaining a deeper understanding of poverty allows teachers to gain a deeper understanding of students who live in poverty.

MAKING IT PERSONAL: POVERTY MURAL

This experiential learning activity is ideally completed with three or four participants. You will work cooperatively to create a mural, drawing from multiple perspectives and multiple perceptions of children living in poverty. Search the Internet using specific terms related to poverty. If needed, ask others for additional key terms related to poverty. Specifically, find and examine:

- Five or more media-based images of children living in poverty
- Three or more recent statistics regarding children living in poverty
- Two or more scholarly articles about children living in poverty
- Two interviews of people with firsthand knowledge of children living in poverty (such as social workers or those who work in social service agencies, food banks, local YMCAs, etc.)

Create a visual representation by blending concepts and ideas gathered from the resources listed above. Synthesize the information you have collected to create one wall-sized mural representing the individual contributions from the members in your group. Consider these questions as you design your mural:

- What is the underlying theme(s) that emerges from your resources?
- What contradictions did you find in the resources?
- In what ways did the information encourage you to think differently about children living in poverty?
- How might you visualize the information?

Once it is completed, present the Poverty Mural to other groups of your peers. As you describe the mural, explain the resources you used and the themes you identified. You may also want to share how the information challenged your preexisting perceptions of children living in poverty or how it created cognitive dissonance within you.

Presenting different perspectives allows you to see poverty from different views. Before starting the Poverty Mural, you had an initial perception of children who live in poverty. This represented your *existing* cognitions. After completing the activity, you gained *new* information from research that may or may not have contradicted your perceptions. Perhaps you experienced cognitive dissonance created by the difference between the old and new knowledge.

UNDERSTANDING THE CONCEPT:
THE COMPLEXITIES OF POVERTY

Similar to the chapter 2 discussion on defining urban, defining poverty can be also be subjective as it may depend on who provides the definition. A person's definition of poverty is often influenced by individual knowledge and experiences. Not everyone experiences poverty and even those who do experience it differently.

Some might say poverty means being poor, but poor is a relative term. A person without a car may be considered poor by some measures, but not to a person without a house. A widely accepted definition of poverty is the inability to provide the basic needs of food, shelter, and clothing. Other definitions suggest poverty is lacking the financial resources to enjoy a minimum standard of living. Understanding what constitutes a minimum standard of living makes the financial definition more comprehensive. Table 3.3 frames poverty from several socioeconomic perspectives related to the standard of living.

Jensen (2009) poses several definitions of poverty, including situational, generational, and relative poverty. These definitions facilitate a deeper understanding of the implications outlined in Table 3.3. Situational poverty is poverty brought on by a catastrophic situation such as illness, disability, natural disaster, or in some cases divorce. Often situational poverty is temporary, but may interrupt the steady flow of family income. For many families losing just one paycheck can have irreversible effects.

Generational poverty refers to families entrenched in poverty for at least two generations. These families do not necessarily have the tools needed to change their situation.

Relative poverty can be seen in families who do not have the means necessary to meet a society's average standard of living. Statistics have shown this to be the most prevalent form of poverty in the United States (Jensen, 2009).

There are multiple risk factors as well as associated implications for children raised in poverty (Brooks-Gunn & Duncan, 1997; Jensen, 2009; Robbins, Stagman, & Smith, 2014). In order to understand the implications in Table 3.3, risk factors must be examined. These risk factors may make daily living a struggle for families and school performance very difficult for many students living in poverty.

Table 3.3.   Socioeconomic Statistics and Implications in the United States

Socioeconomic Statistics	Potential Implication
In the United States federal minimum wage is currently $7.25/hour. The current cost of living is $14.90/hour. (Population in Poverty, 2015)	In order to meet the minimum cost of living, within a household many family members must work more than one job.
According to a 2013 United States Census Bureau report, a family of four living in poverty earns less than $23,550.00/year. (DeNavas-Walt & Proctor, 2015; Measuring Poverty, 2014)	The number of low income working families in the United States increased to 10.4 million in 2011. This means nearly one-third of all working families may not have enough money to meet basic needs.
Nearly one in four children are growing up in poverty. (Individuals Below Poverty Level, 2014)	25 percent of children may not have enough nutritious food to live a healthy life.
Currently, one of every seven households relies on food stamps. One in nine households have a family member who is unemployed or underemployed. (SNAP/Food Stamp Participation Data, 2015; United States Census Bureau, 2014)	By comparison, in the 1970s nearly one out of every fifty Americans relied on food stamps.

Sources: http://www.dol.gov/whd/minwage/america.htm; www.census.gov

Some children are able to rise above all the burdens imposed upon them by poverty. Some are able to focus on their schoolwork and to master whatever assignments they receive. They become excellent students and get high test scores. Some graduate from high school. Some go to college. A few will become highly successful professionals. Most don't. Most are dragged down by the circumstances into which they were born, through no fault of their own (Ravitch, 2013, p. 94).

According to Jensen (2009), the four primary risk factors affecting families living in poverty are: 1) emotional and social challenges, 2) acute and chronic stressors, 3) cognitive lags, and 4) health and safety issues. These risk factors and the implications for children are outlined in Table 3.4.

The factors and implications listed in Table 3.4 are evident in some urban communities across the nation. In these communities, schools are addressing "both the academic and social needs of children" and "doing whatever it takes to obtain the resources and create the conditions to meet and respond to student needs" (Boykin & Noguera, 2011, p. 178).

Table 3.4. Primary Risk Factors of Children Raised in Poverty

Risk Factor	Common Implications
Emotional & Social Challenges	lower school achievement, behavioral problems, grade retention
Acute & Chronic Stressors	hunger, lack of safety, lack of nurturing, malnutrition
Cognitive Lags	developmental delays, learning disabilities, illiteracy
Health & Safety Issues	violence, crime, lead poisoning, lack of health insurance, illness

For example, nutrition programs offered through the schools may have beneficial effects on both physical and cognitive lags for children in poverty. Other schools offer parental education programs, which may also serve to mitigate the risk factors associated with poverty. This is exemplified in Case Study 3.2.

CASE STUDY 3.2: THE BANK STREET SCHOOL

The Bank Street School in New York City is a specific example of a school program in continuous service to an urban community for over ninety-five years. In 1916, an educator named Lucy Sprague Mitchell and her like-minded colleagues examined the current social, educational, economic, and political environment. They concluded creating a new type of educational system was necessary to constructing a "better, more rational humane world" (Bank Street College of Education and School for Children, 2015).

Mitchell, along with Harriet Johnson, and Mitchell's husband, Wesley, founded the Bureau of Educational Experiments, which is now known as Bank Street School. They believed strongly in the revolutionary ideals of John Dewey and other humanists and progressive educators as they sought to discover what kind of environment was best suited to children's learning and growth. Later, they would create the Bank Street College, a graduate program based on their research. This college trains teachers to create and sustain a positive educational environment.

Today, the educational partnership between Bank Street College and Bank Street School for Children is the result of Mitchell's early work.

The School for Children is a nursery through grade eight setting. It includes a family center, which serves infants through nursery school, and is consistent with the social-emotional and developmental approach of the primary school. An on-site medical center helps to address the physical well-being of students. Weekly family programming, including parent education classes and wraparound childcare support, relieves some of the chronic stressors associated with families' abilities to provide infant and early childcare.

This 360-degree offering of support structures, family training, medical services, childhood education, and educator preparation is an outstanding example of how this smaller community of educators continues to serve the larger urban community where Bank Street exists. There is a strong commitment to diversity and inclusive learning opportunities at Bank Street. For young children, parents, and teachers, it is a place where the whole child and, in fact, the whole family is served.

Community partnerships and support for the ideals and practices of Bank Street School for Children and Bank Street College stem from the direct efforts of these educators to assist in reducing the negative effects commonly associated with the four primary risk factors of children living in poverty.

Children and families facing emotional and social challenges, acute and chronic stressors, cognitive lags, and health and safety issues know there are multiple people, programs, and supportive assistance from Bank Street. This support helps to decrease the effects that limit a student's potential and academic promise due to these persistent issues.

CHAPTER SUMMARY

In urban settings many children are impacted by poverty, which may make it difficult for children and their families to meet the most basic needs of food, shelter, clothing, and safety. Maslow studied what drives humans to succeed. He believed people are motivated to fulfill certain levels of need. However, when one need is not met, it may be difficult to meet other needs. Yet children, in spite of daily living challenges that exist, often surpass common expectations.

How can students be ready to learn when many of their primary needs are not being met? The social context of children living in poverty is not insurmountable, but its profound impact cannot be ignored. Understanding the impact of the social context and issues related to poverty affects how teachers view the needs of students, and ultimately how students are effectively taught.

REFERENCES

Bank Street College of Education and School for Children. (2015). *A brief history.* Retrieved from www.bankstreet.edu/discover-bankstreet/what-we-do/history/

Bishaw, A. (2011). Areas with concentrated poverty: 2006–2010. *American community survey briefs.* United States Census Bureau. Retrieved from www .census.gov/prod/2011pubs/acsbr10–17.pdf

Boykin, A. W., & Noguera, P. (2011). *Creating the opportunity to learn: Moving from research to practice to close the achievement gap.* Alexandria, VA: ASCD.

Brooks-Gunn, J., & Duncan, G. (1997). The effects of poverty on children. *The Future of Children, 7*(2), 55–71.

DeNavas-Walt, C., & Proctor, B. (2015). Income and poverty in the United States: 2013. Retrieved from www.census.gov/content/dam/Census/library/publications/2014/demo/p60-249.pdf

Festinger, L. (1957). *A theory of cognitive dissonance.* Stanford: Stanford University Press.

Goldstein, S., & Naglieri, J. (Eds.). (2011). Maslow's Hierarchy of Needs. In *Encyclopedia of child behavior and development* (pp. 913–915). New York: Springer Publishing. DOI: 10.1007/978-0-387-79061-9_1720

Individuals Below Poverty Level. (2014). Retrieved from www.census.gov/search-results.html?q=children being raised in poverty in US&search.x=0&search.y=0&search=submit&page=1&stateGeo=none&searchtype=web

Jensen, E. (2009). *Teaching with poverty in mind: What being poor does to kids' brains and what schools can do about it.* Alexandria, VA: ASCD.

Kincheloe, J. L. (2010). Why a book on urban education? In S. R. Steinberg (Ed.), *19 urban questions: Teaching in the city* (pp. 1–26). New York: Peter Lang Publishing, Inc.

Maslow, A. H. (1943). A theory of human motivation. *Psychological Review, 50*(4), 370.

Measuring Poverty. (2014). National Center for Children in Poverty. Retrieved from www.nccp.org/topics/measuringpoverty.html

Nichols, A. (2013). Poverty in the United States, *Urban Institute Fact Sheet.* www.urban.org/research/publication/poverty-united-states/view/full_report

Population in Poverty. (2014). Kids Count Data Center. Retrieved from www .datacenter.kidscount.org/data/tables/52-population-in poverty?loc=1&loct= 1#detailed/1/any/false/36,868,867,133,38/any/339,340

Prince, D. L., & Howard, E. M. (2002). Children and their basic needs. *Early Childhood Education Journal, 30*(1), 27–31.

Ravitch, D. (2013). *Reign of error: The hoax of the privatization movement and the danger to America's public schools.* New York: Alfred A. Knopf.

Robbins, T., Stagman, S., & Smith, S. (2014). Young children at risk: National and state prevalence of risk factors. Retrieved from www.nccp.org/publications/ pub_1073.html

Schultz, B. D. (2008). *Spectacular things happen along the way.* New York: Teachers College Press.

SNAP/Food Stamp Participation Data 2015. (2015). Retrieved from www.frac .org/reports-and-resources/snapfood-stamp-monthly-participation-data/

United States Census Bureau (2014). Income and poverty in the United States: 2013. Retrieved from www.census.gov/content/dam/Census/library/publica tions/2014/demo/p60-249.pdf

4

Stages of Cognitive Dissonance

Internal Reflections

Essential Question: *In what ways is cognitive dissonance created in teachers whose background is different from that of their students?*

Experiential Learning: *Teachers move through stages of cognitive dissonance in which they question their assumptions and challenge their perceptions of urban schools.*

When people prepare to become teachers they complete a series of requirements gradually building their capacity to plan and implement instruction. For example, individuals preparing to be teachers may start by taking a class on child and adolescent development. They add sophistication to this by learning teaching strategies and applying those to various grade levels or content areas as they plan specific lessons.

The next steps may involve incorporating the needs of individual students, addressing classroom management, and assessing student learning. They are also likely to complete field experiences or practicums as they progressively advance through a program of study.

Most teachers start by observing classroom teachers and students, proceed to tutoring individual or small groups of students, and finally have opportunities to teach larger groups of students. When they successfully navigate these experiences, they move forward to student teaching. It is only after a successful student teaching experience that they are considered ready to assume the full responsibilities of classroom teaching.

It would be unrealistic to expect someone to jump from completing a few simple classroom observations to managing the deep complexities of classroom teaching. Obviously, college coursework and practicums include deliberately designed stages intended to prepare individuals to teach.

The salient point, even if the structure of a specific program varies somewhat from the one described above, is that people move through developmentally sequenced steps as they acquire knowledge and have experiences that prepare them for a teaching career.

UNDERSTANDING THE CONCEPT: STAGES OF COGNITIVE DISSONANCE RELATED TO URBAN SCHOOLS

Like the process of becoming a teacher, cognitive dissonance as it relates to urban schools is also a multistage process. As such, it is unlikely that learning a few isolated facts about urban schools or having one or two experiences within urban schools will adequately build the capacity of teachers to understand and teach the students who attend them.

What pre-service teachers think they know about school, learning, and students (1st cognition) and what they encounter in urban schools (2nd cognition) may be incompatible (dissonance). While this dissonance may be inevitable, it does not need to adversely impact teaching and learning in urban classrooms. Rather, by constantly confronting the dissonance and reflecting on social context and instructional practice, teachers can become more effective in urban classrooms. They can also challenge the political, economic, social, and educational constructs impacting urban students.

As outlined in previous chapters, statistics present the demographic profile of teachers as predominantly white, middle-class, and female. This is a different profile than that of urban students, a majority of whom identify as belonging to racial and ethnic minorities and from families living in poverty (Landsman & Lewis, 2011; Munin, 2012).

The manner in which these two demographic groups experience school and learning can be immensely different. The recognition of this demographic divide and the realization of the challenges it presents is not a recent phenomenon. As early as the 1990s, leading educators identified this demographic imperative as a significant issue for the education profession (Banks, 1995; Dilworth, 1992).

Perhaps a white, female teacher grew up in a middle-class community with little diversity (1st cognition). As an urban teacher, her classroom may be located in a neighborhood with great cultural and linguistic diversity (2nd cognition). The dissonance is created when this teacher thinks, behaves, or responds in ways that support her own experiences, when the actual needs of the students in the classroom are perhaps quite different.

For example, consider a teacher who grew up in a family in which English was the native language. In her urban classroom, many students may come from homes in which English is not spoken. She sends notes home and leaves telephone messages in English, and then wonders why her communication with caregivers is limited. The very recognition of this discord and subsequent reflection presents an opportunity to develop a deeper understanding of herself and a perspective that will increase her ability to become an effective teacher in an urban setting.

Presuming that by philosophically wrestling with a few conflicting beliefs, teachers will suddenly be capable of creating meaningful connections with urban students is a foreshadowing of likely frustration and failure for teachers and students. However, confronting and resolving cognitive dissonance by moving through a series of stages, as depicted in Figure 4.1, may steadily increase the ability of a person to become an effective teacher.

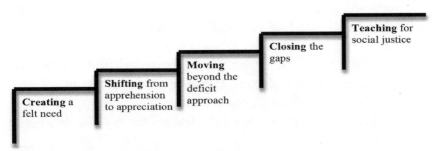

Figure 4.1.   Stages of Cognitive Dissonance

While teachers may move through and between stages at different paces and in different ways, the stages outlined in Figure 4.1 frame this cognitive dissonance as an ongoing developmental journey of discourse rather than a singular consideration of conflicting beliefs. Stages One through Three are introspective and designed to challenge the internal assumptions and perceptions held by individuals. Cognitive dissonance is externalized in Stages Four and Five. The final stages begin to confront practices of social institutions.

Because the final stage includes teaching for social justice, the journey never ends. The *last step* becomes the perpetual *next step* in the constant quest for teachers to construct and reconstruct their understanding of learning and teaching.

In this and the following chapter, each stage of cognitive dissonance is explained in depth. Corresponding experiential learning activities for the stages uncover and challenge common assumptions, beliefs, perceptions, or actions. Stages One through Three, included in this chapter, focus on the assumptions and perceptions an individual may hold. Through a reexamination of current cognitions and the consideration of additional knowledge and information, an individual teacher can move to "new levels of consciousness" (Milner, 2011, p. 60).

Driven by the new level of consciousness, teachers can begin to consider their sphere of influence and move beyond themselves to challenge common systemic practices and policies, which may be deeply embedded with assumptions, beliefs, and perceptions of society. This is the focus of Stages Four and Five, which are outlined in chapter 5.

UNDERSTANDING THE CONCEPT: CREATING THE FELT NEED

Think of a person who is hungry. This person *feels* the need for food because his stomach aches. The ache signals a physiological need for food, and the person attempts to satisfy this need by finding something to eat. Just as people experience physiological needs, they also experience cognitive needs.

In Stage One of cognitive dissonance, a person begins to have a *felt need* to examine a topic or established idea by seeking and analyzing information. A person with a cognitive need seeks out information.

Many teachers feel the need to more fully expand their current understanding of urban schools. They realize there is much more to teaching in urban settings than they may have initially believed. This cognitive dissonance has created a *felt need* for them. Examining and reflecting on this felt need will be an important first step leading to action.

MAKING IT PERSONAL: A KWL CHART ON URBAN SCHOOLS

In this experiential learning activity, you will illustrate a felt need by completing the first two columns of the graphic organizer depicted in Table 4.1. This simple organizer, known as a KWL chart (Ogle, 1986), will help you map what you *Know* (your current cognitions), what you *Want* to know (the dissonance or felt need you are experiencing), and what you hope to *Learn* (your reframed cognitions).

Table 4.1. KWL Chart

K What I *Know* about Urban Schools	W What I *Want* or Need to Know about Urban Schools	L What I Have *Learned* about Urban Schools
Current Cognitions	*Dissonance*	*Change*
1. 2. 3.	1. 2. 3.	1. 2. 3.

As you continue to read this book and complete activities, return back to the chart to add information to the third column and edit information in columns one and two. Understand when you finish reading this book, you are not finished learning. You will constantly be adding and repositioning the information in the chart.

UNDERSTANDING THE CONCEPT: SHIFTING FROM APPREHENSION TO APPRECIATION

Unfortunately, negative stereotypes and characterizations of urban communities frequently create an aura of *apprehension* around urban schools. People unfamiliar with urban communities often draw from media portrayals and information from their families and friends that

present the areas to be dangerous, poorly maintained, and devoid of opportunities and assets.

It is important for teachers to acknowledge the reality for many urban
schoolchildren and their families involves living in a community with
high poverty, crime, and drug use with limited opportunities for meaningful employment or access to healthcare and affordable housing (Welner
& Carter, 2013; Ravitch, 2014). Even advocates of urban education and
children such as William Ayers, Gloria Ladson-Billings, Jonathan Kozol,
H. Richard Milner, and Pedro Noguera (Ayers & Ford, 1996; Ayers,
Ladson-Billings, Michie, & Noguera, 2008; Kozol, 1995; 2005; Milner,
2011; 2013) describe the volatility and desperation that can be found in
urban communities.

Many families and children in urban areas struggle to meet the most
basic physiological needs of food, shelter, and safety. As demonstrated in
Maslow's Hierarchy of Needs, this may impact children's ability to meet
needs related to love and belonging, self-esteem, and self-actualization.
With this in mind, it would be absurd for a teacher not to consider how
these factors impact the school performance of students.

However, it is equally important for teachers to develop an *appreciation* of the unique assets and strengths found within urban communities
and how these support children and families in conjunction with urban
schools. Ladson-Billings (2008) describes a perspective of urban communities, which characterizes them as "vibrant and dynamic" spaces
that include many cultural institutions and practices with the central
mission to promote and support the well-being of children and families
(p. 234). When viewed from this perspective, teachers are able to "locate
the 'good' in social contexts that others have written off as hopeless"
(Milner, 2013, p. 41).

It is possible for people to resituate their view of urban communities.
However, as they create their new consciousness, it is important to resist relying on secondhand, cinematic, literary, or journalistic accounts
of urban communities as the primary sources of information. Rather,
active and personal interactions with urban communities will create the
dissonance needed to trigger the critical paradigm shift from apprehension to appreciation.

MAKING IT PERSONAL: CULTURE WALKS

For those teaching in an urban district, it is important to become familiar with the community surrounding their school. Driving directly from their home to the parking lot of the school and reversing the route at the end of the day will not acquaint them with the surrounding area or help shift their *apprehension* to an *appreciation* of the area.

In this experiential learning activity, you will plan a Culture Walk. Culture Walks are a method for small groups of people to structure meaningful and enlightening interactions within urban communities (Tamura & Others, 1996). They expand the learning environment beyond a college classroom or a textbook and allow you to gain firsthand knowledge in an authentic learning environment—an urban community. However before you start planning your Culture Walk, make a list of words and phrases that come to mind when you think of the urban community you will visit. Save this list for future reference.

Next, research local landmarks, historical sites, long-standing businesses, social service organizations, museums, places of worship, sports associations, and restaurants located within the community. Local business associations and YMCAs, as well as principals, teachers, counselors, and students in a community or neighborhood school can help you identify these establishments. After you complete your research, map a route that will allow you to visit these locations.

Then set aside three to four hours for you and several peers or colleagues to visit as many places as possible. In some communities you may literally walk, while in others you may drive or better yet, take public transportation between the sites. For some locations on your Culture Walk, consider calling in advance of your visit. This will allow you to schedule a time to talk with owners, directors, or other representatives of the organization.

As you visit each stop, note what contributions the organization or business makes to the community. For example, a locally owned bookstore may host poetry slams or highlight authors who have particular relevance to the surrounding community. A museum may offer outreach to schools, and a social service agency may offer tutoring services or help children and families access translation services, housing, or medical care. At each location, spend time talking with people. Introduce yourself and ask them the following questions regarding this community:

- What do you enjoy about this community?
- Why do you choose to work or live here?
- What is a source of pride?
- What two things do you wish people knew about this community?
- What two things are important for teachers to know about children and families who live here?
- What is your vision for this neighborhood?

When you finish your walk, write words and phrases that now come to mind as you think about the community. Compare this to the original list created prior to your Culture Walk. Do you see a shift in the types of words and phrases included in the two lists?

The first list may contain words of *apprehension* reflecting some of the more negative stereotypes of the community. In the second list, you may note words of *appreciation* based on new information you gathered directly from people in the community.

What you previously viewed through a lens of apprehension is now blurred by your experiences of the Culture Walk. This dissonance is an indication you may need to refocus your lens. In doing so, you position yourself to better understand the surroundings of the students in this urban community. The dissonance between *apprehension* and *appreciation* may lead you to change your beliefs about the community and lead you to identify community assets.

UNDERSTANDING THE CONCEPT:
MOVING BEYOND THE DEFICIT APPROACH

In addition to recognizing the assets of urban communities, it is essential to also identify assets of students who attend urban schools. When teachers recognize students' assets or strengths, they can set appropriate expectations for students. Students attending urban schools need teachers who have explicit and high expectations for their students. They do not need well-intended heroic teachers to save them from their surroundings nor do they need teachers who interact with them and their families primarily from a stance of sympathy. While caring for students is important, "it is not enough to be kind and sympathetic" (Nieto, 2010, p. 264).

This rescue mentality or *deficit approach* (Delpit, 1995) implies something is wrong or deficient with urban children, their families, or their communities. As challenging as their lives may be, children living in urban communities do not have inherent deficits.

Teachers who can create caring and trusting classroom environments with clear behavior and academic goals are needed in urban schools. These educators care deeply *and* set high expectations for their students. They work relentlessly to help their students learn *and* accept few excuses from them. They do not avoid teaching rigorous content based on apprehensions and assumptions that urban students bring inadequate prior knowledge or have few resources to contribute to the learning environment. In fact, they realize the surroundings of urban students create unique funds and networks of knowledge that can be developed into rich assets within a classroom (Moll, Amanti, Neff, & Gonzalez, 1992).

Effective urban teachers identify and appreciate the assets of their students and transform these into educational capital. Educational capital is comprised of one or more assets and resources providing the foundation on which to build academic success (Lazar, Edwards, & Thompson McMillon, 2012; Yosso, 2005). Typically educators think of literacy-rich home environments, preschool opportunities, travel, extracurricular activities, educational level of parents, neighborhood stability, and access to adequate housing and healthcare as educational assets.

Urban students, despite the potential for social and economic challenges in their environments, have educational capital that is often overlooked by teachers. Consider the resiliency of urban students. This can be framed as aspirational capital, the desire to maintain and pursue hopes and desires despite hardship.

Many urban students speak multiple languages and/or have heritages rich in storytelling traditions. These assets create linguistic capital. Emotional and educational support can come from extended families that include not just biological relatives but also church or community families. These broaden and enrich the lives of urban students in the form of familial capital.

Finally, the network of urban community resources (similar to those identified in the Culture Walk activity), can be framed as social capital while the ability "to maneuver through social systems" such as schools, governmental bureaucracies, and social service organizations can be viewed as navigational capital (Lazar, Edwards, & Thompson McMillon, 2012, p. 26).

Many people perceive urban students as having limited assets. However, within the social context of urban communities, children and families acquire unique forms of cultural capital (Yosso, 2005). Urban students can draw on this capital to support their education. Examples of the various types of cultural capital held by urban students and their families are provided in Table 4.2.

Table 4.2.   Defining Cultural Capital

cap-i-tal: noun ('ka-pi-tl) an accumulation of valued assets or advantages; synonyms: assets, resources, funds, wealth

Types of Capital:

Aspirational Capital

Lamar's father earned a GED and works two minimum-wage jobs to pay the rent on their run-down rental home. His mother cleans office buildings at night so she can volunteer at Lamar's school and make sure Lamar does well. Still in elementary school, Lamar dreams of graduating from college and becoming a doctor or engineer. He is **aspiring** to a life that will be very different than that of his parents.

Social Capital

Linasha attends a YWCA after school program. Linasha is thirteen and would rather hang out with friends; however, her mother knows Linasha is learning critical college-readiness skills. Her mother has arranged for her brother to participate in their church's mentoring program and for her sister to intern at the Urban League. Linasha and her siblings have a **social network** that will increase their access to information, emotional support, and contacts needed to stay off the streets and in school.

Navigational Capital

Anni's daughter will begin kindergarten in a few months. But Anni does not have insurance to cover the required immunizations or eyeglasses her daughter needs. Anni does not have a computer, making it difficult to complete the school's registration paperwork. When she was teenager and pregnant with her daughter, Anni maneuvered through bureaucratic social service, healthcare, and school systems to acquire resources and finish her GED. Anni can use these same **navigational skills** to access support to prepare her daughter for kindergarten.

cul-tur-al: adjective ('kl-chu-rul, klch-rul)

reflecting traditions, backgrounds, customs, or a way of life; synonyms: contextual, traditional, customary, established

Familial Capital

Czar spent the first three years of his life living with his grandmother. He now lives with his paternal aunt and two cousins. Czar works a part-time job in his uncle's restaurant where another aunt keeps careful watch over him, constantly asking him about his grades or latest girlfriend. His closest friends are two second cousins from his mother's side of the family. He is surrounded by an array of relatives who live in his 'hood. Hardly a weekend goes by without a family barbecue, birthday party, or pickup basketball game. Czar's **extended family** is his most valued asset.

Linguistic Capital

Beshay speaks three languages. His native language is an east African tribal language with a rich storytelling tradition. He learned conversational French during his time in two different refugee camps. He speaks English, his newest language, with some hesitancy and a heavy accent. Despite being nine years old, he interprets for his parents at school, the DMV, in the doctor's office, and with their landlord. Beshay's **language abilities** have given him a wealth of real-world communication skills and helped him develop a social maturity far beyond most of his peers.

Resistance Capital

When Marque was in second grade, her mother convinced the school to provide tutoring rather than place her in a special education program. When she was in sixth grade, her mother was an outspoken critique of a new grading policy. A year later, her mother created an advocacy group to challenge a zero-tolerance discipline plan. Marque, now in high school, contests assignments she views as patronizing and refuses to accept rules she sees as unreasonable. Like her mother, she is highly motivated to **resist** things she perceives to be oppressive or unjust.

The capital students bring to the classroom can serve as a conduit between their lives and the content they are studying. When teachers facilitate the connections between capital and curriculum, urban students are more than capable of meeting academic and behavioral expectations.

Effective urban teachers set high, yet realistic, expectations for their students. They constantly grapple with the dissonance created from an empathetic understanding of the challenges their students face and a firm conviction that their students possess unique educational and cultural capital that can help them meet rigorous expectations.

MAKING IT PERSONAL: COMMON SCENARIOS

Having introduced the concept of capital and knowing the challenges often presented in urban environments, it is time to consider an important balancing act. For each of the scenarios below, take a moment to individually consider how you would determine the appropriate balance between expressing empathy and setting high expectations for students.

Because individual students and their circumstances vary and because behavior will be influenced by the policies and practices of your setting, there are no absolute answers. The value of this experiential learning activity is not to determine a right or wrong approach. Rather, the value of the activity derives from wrestling with the dissonance you feel as you will later explain your responses to the scenarios and questions with a partner or group of peers.

Scenario 1: Some of your students arrive at school hungry, tired, or both. When one of these students lays his or her head on the desk during the first hour of class, will you permit this or will you redirect this behavior?

Scenario 2: Many of your students are unsupervised after school and during the evening. Will you expect them to complete and return homework or will you avoid assigning work outside the school day?

Scenario 3: A majority of your students are reading below grade level. Will you plan literacy lessons that remediate reading skills or will you enrich the existing curriculum with alternative texts?

Scenario 4: It is common for your students to communicate using nonstandard forms of English. Will you correct their use of English or will you allow them to express what they know by using what may be perceived as incorrect English?

Scenario 5: Several of your students respond to conflict by acting aggressively toward their peers. Will you concentrate your efforts to defuse as many student conflicts as possible or will you teach and subsequently expect students to manage their emotions and behavior?

Scenario 6: A prestigious university will be represented at a college fair. Will you encourage students to meet with the recruiter from this university or will you direct them to representatives from more accessible post-secondary options?

Discuss your individual responses to the scenarios with a partner or small group of peers. Remember, there are no absolute right or wrong answers. Use the following questions to facilitate your discussion.

- How does your decision-making represent your dissonance to balance empathy and high expectations for students?
- What information do you have that prompted empathy toward the students?
- What type of educational and cultural capital might apply to each of the scenarios?
- How might the educational and cultural capital of students vary?
- What variables of a school environment might impact your responses to the above scenarios? For example, consider homework policies, emphasis on test scores, or the experience level of an individual teacher.

Each scenario in the activity presented an opportunity to consider real teaching situations with urban students. Teachers must move beyond deficit thinking and set assumptions aside. They must also consider how to balance empathy with expectations and reality with rigor.

Many students come to school as ready learners. They have had a good night's sleep, eaten an ample breakfast, and arrived at school with little stress. This is often not the case in urban areas. Students come to school hungry and tired, feeling the stress of not having these and other needs met.

A teacher's decision-making process needs to be responsive to the students, the day, and/or the assignments rather than an absolute right or wrong. At times, decisions will be heavily influenced by empathy. At other times, decisions will be influenced by high expectations. To be effective in urban environments, teachers must assess each situation in order to provide an appropriate response.

CHAPTER SUMMARY

The initial Stages of Cognitive Dissonance require engagement in a process of introspection to compare what is known with what is not known.

The first three stages of Cognitive Dissonance—creating a felt need, shifting from apprehension to appreciation, and moving beyond a deficit approach—are designed to help teachers challenge their assumptions and perceptions and learn more about students.

As stated in chapter 1, knowing students is a prerequisite for teaching them well. The Culture Walk provided an opportunity to expand learning beyond the classroom and gain firsthand knowledge of the cultural capital that exists in urban communities. The scenario activity connected internal reflections with the broader context of a classroom.

The last two stages of Cognitive Dissonance will be discussed in chapter 5. These stages continue this process, expanding the impact of cognitive dissonance into the classroom, schools, and toward the larger context of society.

REFERENCES

Ayers, W., & Ford, P. A. (Eds.). (1996). *City kids, city teachers: Reports from the front row*. New York: The New Press.

Ayers, W., Ladson-Billings, G., Michie, G., & Noguera, P. (2008). *City kids, city schools: More reports from the front row*. New York: The New Press.

Banks, J. (1995). Multicultural education: Historical development, dimensions, and practice. In J. Banks & C. Banks (Eds.), *Handbook of research on multicultural education* (pp. 3–24). New York: Macmillan.

Delpit, L. (1995). *Other people's children: Cultural conflict in the classroom.* New York: The New Press.

Dilworth, M. (1992). *Diversity in teacher education.* San Francisco: Jossey-Bass.

Kozol, J. (2005). *The shame of the nation: The restoration of apartheid schooling in America.* New York: Crown Publishers.

Kozol, J. (1995). *Amazing grace: The lives of children and the conscience of a nation.* New York: Harper Perennial.

Ladson-Billings, G. (2008). City issues: Beyond the school's walls. In W. Ayers, G. Ladson-Billings, G. Michie, & P. Noguera (Eds.), *City kids, city schools: More reports from the front row* (pp. 225–234). New York: The New Press.

Landsman, J. G., & Lewis, C. W. (Eds.). (2011). *White teachers/diverse classrooms: Creating inclusive schools, building on students' diversity, and providing true educational equity.* Sterling, VA: Stylus Publishing.

Lazar, A. M., Edwards, P. A., & Thompson McMillon, G. (2012). *Bridging literacy and equity: The essential guide to social equity teaching.* New York: Teachers College Press.

Milner, H. R. (2013). *Start where you are, but don't stay there: Understanding diversity, opportunity gaps, and teaching in today's classrooms.* Cambridge, MA: Harvard Education Press.

Milner, H. R. (2011). But good intentions are not enough: Doing what's necessary to teach for diversity. In J. G. Landsman & C. W. Lewis (Eds.), *White teachers/diverse classrooms: Creating inclusive schools, building on students' diversity, and providing true educational equity* (pp. 56–74). Sterling, VA: Stylus Publishing.

Moll, L. C., Amanti, C., Neff, D., & Gonzalez, N. (1992). Funds of knowledge for teaching: Using a qualitative approach to connect homes and classrooms. *Theory into Practice, 31*(2), 132.

Munin, A. (2012). *Color by number: Understanding racism through facts and stats on children.* Sterling, VA: Stylus Publishing.

Nieto, S. (2010). *Language, culture, and teaching: Critical perspectives.* New York: Routledge.

Ogle, D. M. (1986). K-W-L: A teaching model that develops active reading of expository text. *Reading Teacher, 39,* 564–570.

Ravitch, D. (2013). *Reign of error: The hoax of the privatization movement and the danger to America's public schools.* New York: Alfred A. Knopf.

Tamura, L., & Others. (February, 1996). *Preparing teachers to recognize multiple perspectives.* Paper presented at the Annual Meeting of the American Association of Colleges for Teacher Education, Chicago, IL.

Welner, K. G., & Carter, P. L. (2013). Achievement gaps arise from opportunity gaps. In P. L. Carter & K. G. Welner (Eds.), *Closing the opportunity gap: What America must do to give every child an even chance* (pp. 1–10). New York: Oxford University Press.

Yosso, T. J. (2005). Whose culture has capital? A critical race theory discussion of community cultural wealth. *Race, Ethnicity, and Education, 8*(1), 69–91.

5

Stages of Cognitive Dissonance

External Implications

Essential Question: *How can cognitive dissonance created within an individual begin to impact society?*

Experiential Learning: *Teachers move through stages of cognitive dissonance leading them to question policies and practices and teach students to do the same.*

The three stages of cognitive dissonance included in chapter 4 outlined concepts and activities designed to challenge individually held assumptions and perceptions. The two remaining stages of cognitive dissonance, Closing the Gaps and Teaching for Social Justice, are explained in this chapter.

These stages, although intensely personal, extend the impact of cognitive dissonance beyond the individual teacher into the larger context of society. These are critical stages for teachers as "it is important to realize education is part of society. It is not something alien, something that stands outside" of a classroom or school (Apple, 2013, p. 18).

The extension of cognitive dissonance into a wider social context should not intimidate teachers. Yes, confronting broader societal issues is at times difficult and relentless work; it is also highly pragmatic. Cochran-Smith (2004) describes this work as

> profoundly practical in that is it is located in the dailiness of classroom decisions and actions—in teachers' interactions with their students and families,

in their choices of materials and texts, in their utilization of formal and informal assessments, and so on. At the same time, however, it is work that is deeply intellectual in that it involves a continuous and recursive process of constructing understandings, interpretations, and questions (p. 82).

Before learning about Stage Four, Closing the Gaps, complete the following modified Value Line activity (Kagan & Kagan, 2009). This experiential learning activity is designed to examine current cognitions. After developing a deeper understanding related to Stage Four, the activity will be repeated and may provide evidence of changes in beliefs, actions, or perceptions of actions.

MAKING IT PERSONAL: VALUE LINE—PART ONE

To begin this activity, draw a horizontal line on a piece of paper. Label the left end of the line "A" and the right end "O". Mark the center point of the line and five equal increments to the left and right of the center point. The line should resemble Figure 5.1.

Place a paper clip or other small object on the center point. Consider the first pair of statements provided in Figure 5.2 and select either *A* or *O* as the response with which you most agree. If you choose *A*, move the object one increment to the left of the center point. If you choose *O*, move the object one increment to the right of the center point.

Leaving the object in this place, consider the next set of statements. If you choose *A* as the statement with which you most agree, move the object one increment to the left; if you choose *O*, move the object one increment to the right. Repeat this for the remaining statement pairs.

After considering the last set of statements, mark the final location of the object. Save or remember the location of the object; you will refer back to this later. With a partner or small group of peers, compare results and discuss the background information each person contemplated as they selected either *A* or *O* for each pair of statements.

Figure 5.1. Value Line

Pair one - The best way to increase student learning in urban schools is by...	
A	**O**
Retaining experienced teachers who teach in urban schools	Increasing access to quality health care in urban communities

Pair two - The best way to increase student learning in urban schools is by...	
A	**O**
Holding urban school teachers and administrators responsible for advancing student learning	Expanding affordable housing options in urban communities

Pair three - The best way to increase student learning in urban schools is by...	
A	**O**
Extending the length of the school day/year in urban schools	Developing employment opportunities in urban communities

Pair four - The best way to increase student learning in urban schools is by...	
A	**O**
Increasing the number of urban school students who take advanced placement courses	Decreasing the violence and crime in urban communities

Pair five - The best way to increase student learning in urban schools is by...	
A	**O**
Reducing the number of urban school students identified as needing special education support	Improving child care options in urban communities

Figure 5.2.   Value Line Statements

UNDERSTANDING THE CONCEPT: CLOSING THE GAPS

Two persistent, multifaceted gaps, the *achievement gap* and the *opportunity gap*, have permeated urban schools for quite some time. At various times in history, educators, politicians, policy makers, and the media focus their attention on either the achievement gap or opportunity gap. While one gap may be in the spotlight, the other gap remains and may even widen as resources are redirected and reallocated to addressing its counterpart.

The achievement gap refers to a disparity between groups of students based on academic or educational indicators such as standardized test scores (most often those related to literacy, science, and mathematics). On standardized tests, the achievement gap is the difference in academic achievement between high and low performing students. Other educational indicators where gaps exist include enrollment in gifted programs or honors courses, graduation rates, or the percentage of students identified as needing special education support.

Gaps often exist between students who are white and those from racial or ethnic minority groups. Additional gaps may be evident when comparing the gender, ethnicity, or language of student groups. Given the number of groups and number of indicators, it may be more accurate to refer to numerous achievement gaps rather than one distinct achievement gap.

Over the past several decades, achievement gaps have been the center of considerable attention. This attention has, among other things, sparked contentious political and pedagogical debates, increased the amount of testing in P–12 schools, and called into question the ability of urban students as well as the quality and performance of many urban teachers, administrators, and school districts (Ravitch, 2013).

Student achievement differences as determined by test scores are not a new phenomenon. The term *achievement gap* was first used to describe disparities in education-related outcomes as early as the 1960s (Coleman, et al., 1966; Hauser, et al., 1964; Walker, 1963).

Unfortunately, decades of testing data provide evidence of achievement gaps. These gaps have existed historically between white students and students of color, students from affluent backgrounds and students who live in poverty, and native English-speaking students and English-language learners (Ladson-Billings, 2006; Munin, 2012).

It has been important for educators and the public to recognize the achievement disparity between these groups, and certainly the differences are unacceptable. Emphasis on achievement has led to internal and external scrutiny related to educational practices and directed great attention to indicators such as test scores and graduation rates. In fact, the focus on test scores has itself led to the identification of additional gaps related to the educational system such as teacher quality, teacher training, curriculum, and school funding gaps (Irvine, 2010).

Within public education systems, massive resources have been allocated to a) expand educational choices; b) update standards, curriculum, textbooks, and facilities; c) develop and enhance effective teaching practices; d) extend learning time; e) build leadership capacity; and f) improve student outcomes in urban schools (Ravitch, 2014; Welner & Carter, 2013).

Resource allocations by national, state, and local policy makers and school systems are driven by the presumption that educators have significant, if not sole, responsibility for the achievement gaps. Central to this viewpoint is the belief that if educators could just *do more* or *be more effective* the gaps would dissipate.

There is a danger of a perspective centered only on achievement gaps. This limited viewpoint focuses on symptoms rather than causes of performance disparities. This can unfairly target students, teachers, and administrators as bearing primary responsibility for the gaps and label them as underperforming.

As outlined in previous chapters, urban schools have a high percentage of students who live in poverty, identify as racial minorities, and who have a native language other than English. Because of enrollment demographics, these schools educate high numbers of students who often score on the lower end of the achievement spectrum.

In reality, myriad variables entrenched in systems well outside the influence of school systems or a single classroom teacher influence the academic and educational outcomes for urban students. Systemic legislative, judicial, economic, historical, and cultural constructs create intractable learning barriers for many urban school students and their families, leading to overwhelming challenges for urban teachers and administrators. Collectively, these barriers create a very real opportunity gap.

In what ways does achievement of urban students intersect with opportunity? It is important to examine school- *and* community-based

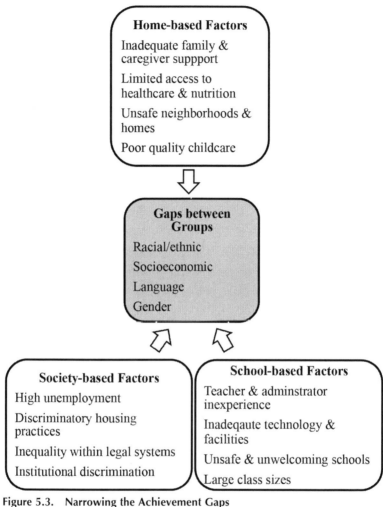

Home-based Factors

Inadequate family & caregiver suppport

Limited access to healthcare & nutrition

Unsafe neighborhoods & homes

Poor quality childcare

Gaps between Groups

Racial/ethnic

Socioeconomic

Language

Gender

Society-based Factors

High unemployment

Discriminatory housing practices

Inequality within legal systems

Institutional discrimination

School-based Factors

Teacher & adminstrator inexperience

Inadeqaute technology & facilities

Unsafe & unwelcoming schools

Large class sizes

Figure 5.3.   Narrowing the Achievement Gaps

resources, as illustrated in Figure 5.3. Societal support for schools, teachers and students, as well as families and communities, is needed if education and achievement gaps are to be narrowed.

The first step to narrowing achievement gaps is to refer to opportunity gaps as well as achievement gaps. While the term achievement gaps focuses on the outcomes of the educational system, the term opportunity gaps draws attention to systems and institutions that influence "key out-of-school factors such as health, housing, nutrition, safety, and enriching life experiences" (Welner & Carter, 2013, p. 3).

The actions, or in some in cases inactions, of social institutions outside of education often create a pattern of intergenerational disparity that "destabilizes children's lives and erodes school achievement" (Kantor & Lowe, 2013, p. 39). In fact they can perpetuate the generational poverty referenced by Jensen (2009). These factors are particularly influential when concentrated in communities and exacerbated by poverty (Rothstein, 2013).

As with the achievement gaps, there is not one distinct opportunity gap. Many urban students are faced with multiple opportunity gaps, each impacting their academic performance. Inequities related to wealth, income, employment, healthcare, nutrition, digital access, adequate housing, and childcare are examples of opportunity gaps prevalent in urban communities (Irvine, 2010).

The focus on opportunity gaps reached a crescendo in the United States in the 1960s. During this era the focus on opportunity gaps was central to a number of federal initiatives. Heavily influenced by President Johnson's Great Society and War on Poverty, the decade saw the passage of civil rights legislation as well as the introduction of a number of social welfare programs. Table 5.1 summarizes several of these initiatives.

Table 5.1.   The Focus on the Opportunity Gaps

Civil Rights Act	Banned employment discrimination based on race and gender; banned segregation in public facilities
Economic Opportunity Act	Strengthened human and financial resources to combat poverty in United States
Fair Housing Act	Protected buyers/renters from discrimination from sellers/landlords
Head Start	Funded preschool education for kindergarten readiness in communities with low socioeconomic levels
Medicaid	Provided health insurance to families/individuals with low incomes/limited resources
Medicare	Provided health insurance for Americans over age sixty-five and also younger people with disabilities
Title 1	Distributed funding to low-income schools and districts through ESEA
VISTA (Volunteers In Service To America)	Provided educational and vocational training programs to people in high-poverty areas through volunteers (domestic Peace Corps)
Voting Rights Act	Prohibited racial discrimination in voting

This is not to discount the significant events related to the nation's educational system. In addition to the social legislation of the 1960s, the federal government increased its efforts to enforce the 1954 Supreme Court ruling in the *Brown v. Board of Education* Topeka school deseg-regation case.

Congress also enacted the 1965 Elementary and Secondary Educa-tion Act (ESEA), which included funding via Title I provisions for low-income and urban students. Bilingual and higher education legislation were also part of the educational legacy of the 1960s.

Just as an achievement-only perspective has its downfall, so too does an opportunity-only perspective. A fixation on issues external to schools may minimize the profound impact schools and teachers have on students. It is also plausible that some educators may use opportunity gaps as an excuse for setting low expectations for urban students or for justifying their own poor teaching performance.

Efforts tied to the achievement perspective, such as increasing and re-taining well-prepared teachers, improving the quality of instruction, and delivering a challenging curriculum in urban schools are critical. This is important not just to improve test scores, but to also dismantle the social and economic obstacles that lead to the opportunity gaps.

Educators can address both the achievement and opportunity gaps by resisting a single focus on achievement gaps that frame urban districts as failing, teaching in urban schools as a Herculean task where few find success and fulfillment, and urban students as somehow intellectually deficient. Equally important is resisting a single focus on the opportunity gaps that can minimize the important influence of adequate resources in urban schools, quality teachers who set high expectations, and the cultural capital of urban students.

Developing an understanding of both perspectives is essential. For example, individuals may originally focus on the achievement gaps (1st cognition), and then expand their knowledge by learning more about op-portunity gaps (2nd cognition). They begin to realize they didn't know what they didn't know (dissonance). This dissonance allows them to reconstruct their knowledge about opportunities and obstacles faced by urban schools. Considering both perspectives challenges and expands the existing knowledge base of educators.

MAKING IT PERSONAL: VALUE LINE—PART TWO

Review the final location of the object on the Value Line—Part One activity. If the object was closer to the *A*, you may have been focusing on factors often associated with the achievement gaps as you reflected on your choices. If the object was closer to the *O*, you may have been centering your decisions based on factors related to the opportunity gaps.

Based on what you learned regarding the achievement and opportunity gaps, repeat the Value Line activity. Compare the final location of the object from the first to second completion of the activity and consider the following:

- If there was a change, what led to the change?
- What does the location of the object reveal in terms of additional or new information you may need to better understand the complexities of achievement gaps, opportunity gaps, or both?
- How are the gaps connected?
- How does knowledge of the achievement and opportunity gaps impact Stage Two, Shifting from Apprehension to Appreciation, and Stage Three, Moving Beyond the Deficit Approach?

UNDERSTANDING THE CONCEPT: TEACHING FOR SOCIAL JUSTICE

The achievement and opportunity gaps discussed in Stage Four are the results of inequities. Social justice is a philosophical perspective that directs individuals to act in a manner leading to a more just or equitable world. The idea that deep-seated institutional injustices exist in many facets of society is a central concept of social justice philosophy (Rawls, 1971).

These injustices are manifested in practices and policies that often go unnoticed or seem innocuous to some individuals, but have a profound negative impact on others. When these inequities are viewed through the social justice lens, people recognize they can and should use their positions to challenge unfair social systems.

Social justice is applied to many areas, including medicine, housing, political engagement, social work, criminal justice, and education. An example can be seen in reviewing the voting rights of African Americans in the United States from the perspective of social justice. In 1870, the 15th Amendment to the Constitution of the United States gave African Americans the right to vote.

Despite this legal right, many ingrained systemic inequities remained after the passage of the amendment. These systemic practices prevented African Americans from voting. For example, the process of registering to vote required African Americans to travel to areas where they did not feel safe. In other places, African Americans were required to take oaths or pledges not required of other voters.

Voter registration practices were oppressive to African Americans, but viewed as routine and acceptable by many white Americans. The realization of these social injustices spurred many others to take action. While some people took action by engaging in concerted efforts to register African American voters in the South, others took action through protests and demonstrations.

The Voting Rights Act of 1965 passed as a response to these injustices as well as the actions of those who had advocated for change. Even beyond this legislation, people continued to suffer injustice within the American legal system. Though many celebrated the passage of the Voting Rights Act, injustices related to voting remain. Efforts to challenge systemic practices that continue to suppress the African American voters are part of the ongoing social justice movement in the United States.

Teaching from a social justice perspective means teachers continually question their existing assumptions about difference, privilege, and culture (Cochran-Smith, 2004). It is a recursive process in which teachers examine their own experiences and the experiences of others. Socially just teachers actively and intentionally seek the perspectives of others, particularly those who may be marginalized by society (Lalas, 2007).

In doing so, teachers' current knowledge (1st cognition) is challenged as they began to notice and learn about the inequalities of society and particularly how these may be manifested in a school or classroom environment (2nd cognition).

The dissonance between the two conflicting cognitions leads teachers to a key component of social justice—*action*. Socially just teachers go beyond knowledge and take personal, social, and civic actions leading to more democratic and equitable classrooms, schools, and communities. They also teach their students about social injustices. Not only do they help students understand social injustice, they intentionally provide opportunities for students to learn the critical thinking, collaborative, and communications skills needed so they too can challenge inequities.

MAKING IT PERSONAL:
TEACHING FOR SOCIAL JUSTICE GALLERY WALK

In this experiential learning activity, you will examine an issue through the lens of social justice. Follow the steps outlined below to help you analyze and present a social issue.

1. Identify a social inequity. Consider one of your own choosing, or draw from the areas of immigration, healthcare, gay rights, criminal justice, education, income inequality, or social welfare.
2. Who is negatively impacted by this inequity in society or your specific community?
3. What groups of students may be negatively impacted by this inequity in a classroom, school, or school district?
4. Who may potentially be unable to see this as a problem?
5. As an educator, what possible actions can you take to address this injustice?
6. What would you hope to be the result of those actions?

Review several credible resources related to your topic. Include news sources and scholarly articles. After you have reviewed this information, discuss what you learned with several peers and ask for their input or perspectives. Develop and synthesize your position related to the issue. Articulate this position by creating a teaching for social justice poster professionally presenting information from your research.

Share the poster with your peers through a Gallery Walk. A Gallery Walk (Kagan & Kagan, 2009) is a simple and effective way to view multiple posters and discuss several social justice issues.

The steps for creating a Gallery Walk include:

1. Display posters around the perimeter of the room. Keep in mind the importance of an eye-level approach when hanging or arranging your posters.
2. Post a brief summary of key points and author's intentions close to each poster. This allows observers to both visually and cognitively interact with the poster.
3. Assign small groups of individuals, or even pairs, to begin at one specific poster. Each group/pair begins at a different poster.
4. Time the Gallery Walk so observers spend approximately five to ten minutes to view and discuss each poster.
5. Ring a bell or chime at the end of the five to ten minutes to signal each group/pair to walk to the next poster. Clockwise or counter-clockwise rotations easily manage the transitions. At the second location, groups or pairs will spend another five to ten minutes viewing and discussing the next poster.
6. The process continues until each group has read each of the posters.

The Gallery Walk provides an opportunity to examine several social justice issues. Individuals gain a perspective on issues that are meaningful to them, as well as how these issues are framed through the social justice lens. This provides a foundation to examine other social justice issues related to urban education.

CHAPTER SUMMARY

Stages Four and Five were designed to externalize cognitive dissonance as it relates to teaching in urban settings. Once teachers challenge their own assumptions and perceptions, they can then begin to challenge similar issues within the broader community. This relates to the sphere of influence in chapter 2 and will be discussed further in chapter 6.

As it applies to urban schools, cognitive dissonance is structured in five stages. Some stages will resonate more strongly with one person than other stages. Likewise, some people may find stronger connection with a certain stage than other people. It is also possible after completing activities related to one of the stages, people may begin to reconsider previous stages. This is precisely what is intended.

Cognitive dissonance is an ongoing process unique to individuals. A teacher may move through, as well as between, the stages at various points in his or her career. The final stage of cognitive dissonance, teaching for social justice, is further explored in the following chapter.

REFERENCES

Apple, M. W. (2013). *Can education change society?* New York: Routledge Publishing.

Cochran-Smith, M. (2004). *Walking the road: Race, diversity, and social justice.* New York: Teachers College Press.

Coleman, J. S., Campbell, E. Q., Hobson, C. J., McPartland, J., Mood, A. M., Weinfeld, F. D., et al. (1966). *Equality of educational opportunity.* Washington, DC: U.S. Department of Health, Education, and Welfare.

Hauser, P. M., McMurrin, S. M., Nabrit, J. M., Nelson, L. W., & Odell, W. R. (1964). *Integration of the public schools—Chicago.* Chicago, IL: Board of Education, Chicago Public Schools.

Irvine, J. J. (2010). Foreword in H. R. Milner (Ed.), *Culture, curriculum, and identity in education* (pp. xi–xv). New York: Palgrave Macmillan.

Jensen, E. (2009). *Teaching with poverty in mind: What being poor does to kids' brains and what schools can do about it.* Alexandria, VA: ASCD.

Kagan, S., & Kagan, M. (2009). *Kagan Cooperative Learning.* San Clemente, CA: Kagan Publishing.

Kantor, H., & Lowe, R. (2013). Educationalizing the welfare state and privatizing education: The evolution of social policy since the New Deal. In P. L. Carter & K. G. Welner (Eds.), *Closing the opportunity gap: What America must do to give every child an even chance* (pp. 25–39). New York: Oxford University Press.

Ladson-Billings, G. (2006). From the achievement gap to the education debt: Understanding achievement in U.S. schools. *Educational Researcher, 35*(7), 3–12.

Lalas, J. (2007). Teaching for social justice in multicultural urban schools: Conceptualization and classroom implication. *Multicultural Education, 14*(3), 17–21.

Munin, A. (2012). *Color by number: Understanding racism through facts and stats on children.* Sterling, VA: Stylus Publishing.

Ravitch, D. (2013). *Reign of error: The hoax of the privatization movement and the danger to America's public schools.* New York: Alfred A. Knopf.

Rawls, J. (1971). *A Theory of Justice.* Cambridge, MA: Harvard University Press.

Rothstein, R. (2013). Why children from lower socioeconomic classes, on average, have lower academic achievement than middle-class children. In P. L. Carter & K. G. Welner (Eds.), *Closing the opportunity gap: What America must do to give every child an even chance* (pp. 61–74). New York: Oxford University Press.

Walker, G. (1963, July 6). Englewood and the northern dilemma. *The Nation, 197*, 7–10.

Welner, K. G., & Carter, P. L. (2013). Achievement gaps arise from opportunity gaps. In P. L. Carter & K. G. Welner (Eds.), *Closing the opportunity gap: What America must do to give every child an even chance* (pp. 1–10). New York: Oxford University Press.

6

Transforming Knowledge into Action

Essential Question: *How can personal knowledge transform into professional action?*

Experiential Learning: *Action must be based on knowledge. It is not enough to know; teachers must now act!*

In Cognitive Dissonance Theory, Festinger (1957) suggested three ways to resolve dissonance: changes in beliefs, changes in actions, and changes in perceptions of actions. At first, changing beliefs may seem the simplest way to resolve dissonance. Yet other options can be considered.

For example, a man might have a conversation with himself over cheating on a diet. If he were to decide to change his beliefs, he might say, *"It's okay to cheat."* If he decided to cheat on this diet, he might resolve his dissonance by saying he will never cheat again or he will resume his diet tomorrow. *"Even though yesterday I ate donuts, it's okay because today I have not eaten donuts."* This is a change in his actions. If he decided to cheat on this diet, he might resolve his feelings by saying, *"It's okay to cheat because everyone else is cheating."* He reframes his actions in a different context, so his actions do not conflict with his beliefs. This is a change in perceptions of his actions.

In previous chapters, experiential learning activities and discussions guided the process of cognitive dissonance related to urban schools. What teachers thought they knew about themselves and urban students may have been challenged with new information. This may have resulted in dissonance to be resolved. Considering Festinger's resolutions, how can cognitive dissonance be transformed into action in urban schools?

UNDERSTANDING THE CONCEPT: TEACHERS AS ACTIVISTS

The call for teachers to take actions that address social inequities is not new or limited to the Theory of Cognitive Dissonance. In past centuries, prominent educators such as W. E. B. Du Bois (1868–1963), Paulo Freire, (1921–1997), Howard Zinn (1921–1997), and others have implored teachers to expand their sphere of influence beyond the academic achievements of their students.

Du Bois focused his attention on systemic oppression of people of color, and Freire concentrated his efforts on institutional oppression of the poor. Zinn focused on incorporating the voices of marginalized populations into the curriculum. All three called for teachers to take action and become activists within their classrooms and communities. They were "critical scholar/activists" who challenged teachers to question socially unjust policies and practices within their buildings, their profession, their communities, and broader society (Apple, 2013, p. 22).

As teachers examine the people and places surrounding them, they may wonder how issues of injustice are manifested in their contexts. It may not be immediately evident where and how social injustice occurs within education. Yet thinking and exploring inequities, both small- and large-scale, provides teachers opportunity to reexamine experiences extending beyond their classrooms.

To explore inequities in education, teachers should understand how students experience school in different ways. For example, consider an analysis of the literature selected in schools' curricula. The fictional characters presented in children's literature in American curriculums do not reflect the real world's diversity (Horning, Lindgren, & Schliesman, 2013). As such, some students may never see themselves accurately reflected in school reading material. This may impact their connection to school and the development of a positive cultural identity (Lazar, Edwards, & Thompson McMillon, 2012).

Recognizing issues of inequity exist is the precursor to questioning social injustices in and outside the classroom. When a teacher applies a social justice perspective to a classroom, important considerations emerge. The first question to consider is, *How does social justice impact the classroom actions of a teacher?* If principles of social justice are embedded in teaching philosophies, teachers take action and create opportunities to incorporate authentic social issues into their teaching and professional work.

As teachers move through the Stages of Cognitive Dissonance, they become well-prepared to apply what they have learned about their students to teaching practices. They can supplement classroom materials with resources reflecting the rich diversity and backgrounds of their students, and purposefully select social topics relevant to their students.

For example, in a mathematics unit on graphing, a teacher could assign students to create graphs depicting the number of grocery stores or public recreation areas in various parts of the city. As they learn the mathematical process by graphing the data related to these topics, students may also discover differences between neighborhoods.

Initially, this creates an opportunity for the class to have discussions about concepts of graphing. Subsequently, the class can discuss how access to grocery stores selling nutritional food and places for children to spend time playing outdoors varies between communities. Connecting curriculum and the social context of urban students has the potential to increase student engagement and lead to discussions about differences and why such social inequities may exist.

Consider another opportunity in the area of social studies. When teaching elementary or secondary students how a bill becomes a law, a teacher can select a signature piece of civil rights legislation to follow through the legislative process. For younger children, this not only serves as a source of information about how a bill becomes a law, but also provides a model of how discriminatory social structures are challenged and changed.

As older students examine a particular piece of civil rights legislation, topics of civil resistance, political compromises, and unintended consequences will help them understand not only the Constitutional concept of checks and balances but also the complexities of the social change process.

A second question for consideration is, *How can social justice impact the actions of students?* In other words, how can a teacher equip students with the skills and confidence so they become activists rather than passive "completers of tasks and recipients of grades?" (Peterson, 2001, p. 221). Teachers extend their sphere of influence when they prepare students to "take what they learn back to their homes and neighborhoods in the form of new understanding and new behavior" and use knowledge and skills to challenge inequities (Karp, 2007, p. 189). In essence, students are taught how to "talk back to the world" (Teachers for Social Justice, 2006).

To prepare students to take these types of actions, they need to be taught to think critically, analyze information, synthesize ideas, and develop informed opinions related to social topics. They also need to develop and practice their collaborative skills, as well as their abilities to articulate and debate their points of view. Impacting the actions of students is an extension of the sphere of influence of a teacher.

The curriculum provides many opportunities to integrate these skills with social justice topics relevant to urban students. For example, during writing instruction, an elementary or secondary teacher can teach students how to identify credible evidence, form an opinion, and articulate a position. Students can then complete research, appropriate to their grade and ability level, on topics closely related to their social context such as access to technology, employment opportunities, housing, or healthcare.

Combining critical thinking skills with research, students can complete assignments requiring them to write persuasive letters to the editor of the local newspaper, elected representatives, or school administrators. In these letters, students not only demonstrate persuasive writing skills, but they also advocate for social change.

MAKING IT PERSONAL:
IMAGINING A SOCIALLY JUST CLASSROOM

In this experiential learning activity, imagine an elementary or secondary classroom, perhaps one you have visited recently. Picture the materials and resources in that classroom. What were students doing in the classroom? What were the teachers doing? Based on your recollection, consider Table 6.1 and discuss to what extent these components were evident in this classroom.

Not all teachers approach social justice in the same way. However, Table 6.1 represents elements commonly found in the classrooms of

Table 6.1. Components of a Socially Just Classroom

The classroom:	The students:	The teacher:
displays the work of students.	feel safe & cared for by teacher & peers.	makes certain students learn about each other.
arrangement is conducive to discussions.	collaborate with peers, teachers, & other adults.	invites other adults into the classroom.
resources reflect the lives of students.	have a voice in the learning process.	values students' knowledge & input.
represents many cultures & perspectives.	ask critical questions about relevant issues.	ties significant issues to multiple subjects.
learning tasks represent appropriate academic rigor.	hold peers to high academic expectations.	poses intellectually rigorous questions.
curriculum embeds social issues into projects & assessments.	are assessed in multiple ways & encouraged to assess their own work.	uses a variety of performance & project-based assessments.
materials are critically analyzed by teachers & students.	appropriately question policies & challenge ideas.	models critical inquiry within the school setting.

teachers who have a social justice perspective (Au, Bigelow, & Karp, 2007; Cochran-Smith, 2004). Rather than focusing solely on what social justice *looks like*, it is important to also consider how teachers "struggle to think about and understand what they are doing" (Cochran-Smith, 2004, p. 82).

Consider these questions:

- How have your previous understandings of classroom resources, students, and teachers (1st cognition) been challenged by the concept of social justice teaching (2nd cognition)?
- After reviewing the items in Table 6.1, in what ways might you change or reconsider the vision of your classroom (dissonance)?
- What *actions* might you need to take in order to increase the social justice focus within your classroom?

In chapter 2, the general concept of sphere of influence was introduced. In this chapter, you will personalize the concept. Actions in and beyond the

classroom are part of your *personal* sphere of influence as a teacher. The
ways in which you choose to interact within the boundaries of your sphere
of influence become your personal sphere of influence as a teacher.

UNDERSTANDING THE CONCEPT: PERSONAL SPHERE OF INFLUENCE MODEL

Recognizing inherent differences in life experiences leads to a discussion
of personal influence and locus of control. Both are components within a
personal sphere of influence. As outlined in chapter 2, the general sphere
of influence involves people and places who influence someone's ideas
and experiences, and shape *that* person's understandings, beliefs, and
achievements. Concurrently, that person also contributes to the spheres of
influence of others, including the shaping of *their* understandings, beliefs,
and achievements.

   A personal sphere of influence is characterized by the ways in which a
person chooses to act within and among the layers of her home, school,
and community. It places self at the center of all this action, and is different from the general sphere of influence due to the focus on personal
actions. Figure 6.1 illustrates the personal sphere of influence.

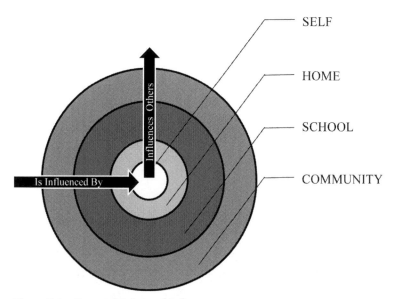

Figure 6.1.   Personal Sphere of Influence

Recognizing the elements one can control or influence, compared to elements one cannot, establishes a person's locus of control and their resulting abilities to act. Teachers have limited or no control over some aspects of their professional life, such as the family income of their students or the physical condition of their school. However, teachers do have control over other aspects of their professional life, such as their classroom expectations and the teaching strategies they utilize. Identifying their locus of control is an important step in learning how to effectively navigate and influence their immediate environments.

The classroom serves as a contextual opportunity for teachers to act within their personal spheres of influence. Teachers' values and cultural backgrounds influence interactions with students as well as the manner in which teachers present academic content. Likewise, students influence teachers. Students' values and cultural backgrounds influence interactions and the knowledge and capital they bring into the classroom.

Teachers' values and backgrounds may lead to unrecognized biases that manifest in classrooms and schools. While many people make assumptions that schools and classrooms are equitable and unbiased environments, "schools have never been value-free. Politics, culture, and ideology shape all aspects of school life—from teachers' favoritism toward some students to unexamined premises guiding curriculum" (Au, Bigelow, & Karp 2007, p. 145).

Figure 6.1 illustrates that people and places influence one another. Personal spheres of influence are different for individuals because life experiences of one may be dramatically different from those of another. As one encounters opportunities and obstacles in life, one's ability to act within a personal sphere of influence flexes over time to accommodate specific people, places, and experiences.

MAKING IT PERSONAL: IDENTIFYING ELEMENTS IN YOUR PERSONAL SPHERE OF INFLUENCE

Consider social interactions and influences within *your* immediate environment by identifying people, places, and events that influence you. These individual elements combine to create *your* sphere of influence. The process of identifying your personal sphere of influence enables you to become a participant in social change.

In this experiential learning activity you will work individually to identify specific elements within your sphere of influence and respond to the following questions:

- Who and what influences you at home, school, the workplace and/ or community?
- How do these people, places, and events impact you?
- Who and what important people and places from your past have impacted you?
- How have you been influenced by people, places, and events from your past?
- In what ways do you presently influence other people, places, and events?

Based on these responses, create a visual representation of your sphere. If you are comfortable, share this with classmates, friends, peers, colleagues, and/or family.

While the first part of this activity is individual and internally driven, the next part is externally driven. Beyond the classroom setting, but within your sphere of influence:

- What do you see that you would like to change?
- Where do you have the power to make something better?
- How can you influence social change? (Doerr, 2010)

By creating your personal sphere of influence you now have a platform from which to identify areas of needed social change. This guides your personal actions as you become a catalyst for change beyond the classroom.

CHAPTER SUMMARY

Becoming a teacher for social justice is immensely personal and ongoing. It is a process of cycling and recycling through the stages of cognitive dissonance as it relates to urban schools. It is a constant and recurrent process of building new knowledge, questioning existing knowledge, and taking action within a personal sphere of influence.

The classroom practices of teachers with a social justice perspective are guided by a belief that teaching can influence social change and address inequities. Teachers believe the actions they take influence their students both academically and socially.

The impact of socially just teachers is exponential. It reaches beyond teaching content and skills and enables students to challenge social injustices. Imagine the power of one teacher's personal sphere of influence extended to twenty-five individual students. Each of those twenty-five students uses what they have learned and takes action within their personal spheres of influence.

Teachers who engage their profession from a social justice perspective take action when they scrutinize policies and practices within their schools. Further, they utilize their influence to question and challenge systemic policies and practices that may be inequitable for the students in their classrooms, schools, or districts.

REFERENCES

Apple, M. W. (2013). *Can education change society?* New York: Routledge Publishing.

Bigelow, B., Harvey B., Karp, S., & Miller, L. (2001) *Rethinking our classrooms: Teaching for equity and justice, Volume 2.* Milwaukee, WI: Rethinking Schools, Ltd.

Cochran-Smith, M. (2004). *Walking the road: Race, diversity, and social justice.* New York: Teachers College Press.

Doerr, E. (2010). What is social change? In W. Wagner, D. T. Ostick, & S. R. Komives (Eds.), *Leadership for a better world: Instructor's manual* (pp. 10–31). San Francisco: Jossey-Bass.

Festinger, L. (1957). *A theory of cognitive dissonance.* Stanford: Stanford University Press.

Horning, K. T., Lindgren, M. V., & Schliesman, M. (2013). A few observations on publishing in 2012. *CCBC Choices 2013.* Madison, WI: Cooperative Children's Book Center.

Karp, S. (2007). Why we need to go beyond the classroom. In W. Au, B. Bigelow, & S. Karp (Eds.), *Rethinking our classrooms: Teaching for equity and justice, Volume 1, New edition* (pp. 188–193). Milwaukee, WI: Rethinking Schools, Ltd.

Lalas, J. (2007). Teaching for social justice in multicultural urban schools: Conceptualization and classroom implications. *Multicultural Education, 14*(3), 17–21.

Lazar, A. M., Edwards, P. A., & Thompson McMillon, G. (2012). *Bridging literacy and equity: The essential guide to social equity teaching.* New York: Teachers College Press.

Levine, J. H. (1972). The sphere of influence. *American Sociological Review, 37*(1), 14–27. Retrieved from www.dartmouth.edu/~jlevine/Sphere%20of%20 Influence%20Levine.pdf

Peterson, B. (2001). Motivating students to do quality work. In W. Au, B. Bigelow, & S. Karp (Eds.), *Rethinking our classrooms: Teaching for equity and justice, Volume 2* (pp. 219–224). Milwaukee, WI: Rethinking Schools, Ltd.

Teachers for Social Justice (2006). Working principles. Retrieved from: www .teachersforjustice.org/2006/06/working-principles.html

7

Translating Theory into Action

Cognitive dissonance is a common thread in this book. Confronting incompatible ideas (cognitions) may lead to resolving dissonance through what Festinger (1957) identified as changes in beliefs, changes in actions, or changes in perceptions of actions. Opportunities to confront and resolve dissonance may present themselves unexpectedly. It is important for teachers to seize these opportunities in order to better understand and serve students in urban classrooms.

A second common thread of this book is sphere of influence. The actions of individuals may greatly impact some people within their spheres. Inactions may influence other people. A third common thread throughout the book is social justice, which challenges teachers to take action and extend their sphere of influence.

The following case study presents an example of how several individuals confronted a social issue. The role of each person in this case study is explained to further exemplify cognitive dissonance, sphere of influence, and social justice.

CASE STUDY 7.1: RUBY BRIDGES

On the morning of November 16, 1960, two federal marshals escorted a young girl into William Frantz Elementary School in New Orleans, Louisiana. A large crowd gathered to witness Ruby Bridges be the first

African American student to attend an all-white elementary school in New Orleans, after a federal judge had ordered the desegregation of schools.

The crowd in front of the school was volatile, later turning violent, shouting obscenities, and threatening death to Ruby and her family. Many parents chose to remove their children from the school, refusing to have them attend with an African American student. A teacher, Barbara Henry, was hired to teach Ruby, who was the only student in her first-grade classroom.

In Ruby's second year of school, federal marshals had left, as had the protestors and Mrs. Henry. More and more African American students attended Frantz and many white students returned to the school.

The details of this story exemplify Ruby Bridges' personal sphere of influence. Ruby's mother wanted her to receive an education in the same school as white children. This represents the influence of her home.

> Ruby was special. I wanted her to have a good education so she could get a good job when she grew up. But Ruby's father thought his child shouldn't go where she wasn't wanted.

> There were things I didn't understand. I didn't know Ruby would be the only black child in the school. I didn't know how bad things would get. I remember being afraid on the first day Ruby went to the Frantz School, when I came home and turned on the TV set and I realized that, at that moment, the whole world was watching my baby and talking about her. At that moment, I was most afraid" (Lucille Bridges, as cited in Bridges, 1999, p. 12).

Her teacher significantly shaped Ruby's experience at school. "I know now that Mrs. Henry influenced me a great deal that year . . . In fact I began to imitate her." (Ruby Bridges, as cited in Bridges, 1999, p. 14).

This relationship was not one-sided, as Mrs. Henry also spoke of *her* relationship with Ruby. "I grew to love Ruby and to be awed by her. It was an ugly world outside, but I tried to make our world together as normal as possible" (Barbara Henry, as cited in Bridges, 1999, p. 23). The relationship between Ruby Bridges and Mrs. Henry represents the influence of the school.

Ruby Bridges' personal sphere of influence extended beyond the classroom, as her actions forever changed the landscape of public education in New Orleans and across the country. This represents her influence on her community. On that day in 1960, Ruby Bridges just wanted to go to school. She did not consider that her actions would become a historic moment for public schools in the United States. In her words:

> Though I did not know it then, nor would I come to realize it for many years, what transpired in the fall of 1960 in New Orleans would forever change my life and help shape a nation. When I think back on that time and all that has occurred since, I realize a lot has changed. I also know there is much more to be done. That fateful walk to school began a journey, and we all must work together to continue moving forward (Ruby Bridges as cited in Bridges, 2013).

The details of this case study also provide an example of Cognitive Dissonance. Consider the story of Mrs. Henry. Years after her time at William Frantz Elementary School, she stated, "I thought New Orleans would be a romantic place, filled with southern hospitality" (1st cognition) (Barbara Henry, as cited in Bridges, 1999, p. 43).

After agreeing to teach an integrated class at Frantz, Mrs. Henry soon realized there were implications of teaching this class, which turned out to include only Mrs. Henry and Ruby. Not only were angry mobs using hateful words and threatening violence against Ruby, Mrs. Henry faced hostility from her colleagues. "When I went to the teachers' lounge at lunchtime, the other teachers at first ignored me or made unpleasant remarks about the fact that I was willing to teach a black child" (Barbara Henry, as cited in Bridges, p. 43).

New Orleans was not full of southern hospitality, and its schools were vastly different than the integrated schools in Boston where Mrs. Henry previously taught (2nd cognition). Despite this new knowledge, she was unwilling to give up on Ruby, even with underlying tones of fear and intimidation looming over their classroom.

With her previous image of New Orleans clashing with the current reality of her experiences in Frantz Elementary School, Mrs. Henry was forced to resolve the dissonance she was experiencing. She could change her beliefs, change her actions, or change the perceptions of her actions. She chose to take action.

Despite having only one student in her classroom, Mrs. Henry created meaningful learning experiences for Ruby. Because Ruby was not allowed on the playground, Mrs. Henry made certain Ruby was able to get physical activity within the classroom. She chose to eat lunch with Ruby, since Ruby was prohibited from the lunchroom.

Mrs. Henry's actions extended beyond her classroom and interactions with Ruby. She defended Ruby when the principal threatened to change the grades Ruby had earned. The principal told her Ruby had received too much individual attention, rendering the grades as inaccurate. It is unknown whether Mrs. Henry's actions resulted in grade changes. Ruby resolved this by saying, "It didn't matter. The principal couldn't change what was in my head" (Ruby Bridges, as cited in Bridges, 1999, p. 50).

When four white first-grade students began attending Frantz in the spring of 1961, Mrs. Henry demanded they spend time with Ruby. The principal was reluctant to do so until Mrs. Henry reminded the principal of the law regarding integration and threatened to report this to the superintendent.

Mrs. Henry's story further exemplifies the concept of personal sphere of influence. Mrs. Henry leveraged her personal sphere of influence within the school to help Ruby feel safe and to learn. It also extended beyond the school. "Over the years, I told my children about her again and again. I had to keep the memory alive" (Barbara Henry, as cited in Bridges, 1999, p. 52).

Her bravery, compassion, and determination to protect Ruby from the injustices of segregation were admirable. "I didn't want to allow hate to enter her life and in any way diminish her beautiful spirit" (Barbara Henry, as cited in Bridges, 1999, p. 44). This represents her influence beyond her community. Mrs. Henry's role in Ruby Bridges' life and historic place in the civil rights movement remain part of the story that forever changed the landscape of public education.

School segregation was and continues to be a social justice issue challenging the United States. The actions taken by Ruby Bridges, her mother, and Mrs. Henry forced Americans to rethink their beliefs and attitudes regarding privilege and inequality in public education. Although their actions started as a small personal step, they quickly extended into their local community, and eventually impacted inequities in education throughout the country.

Like Mrs. Henry, teachers are often confronted with situations in which beliefs about students will conflict with a particular school policy. These incompatible ideas will require resolution. Mrs. Henry exemplifies how teachers can challenge the policies and change their actions in order to support their students.

As this book has outlined, cognitive dissonance, personal sphere of influence, and social justice are important concepts for teachers especially as they pertain to teaching in urban environments. Cognitive dissonance and sphere of influence provide a foundation for teaching for social justice. Linda Darling-Hammond (2002) describes the intersection of these three concepts.

> Learning to teach for social justice is a lifelong undertaking. It involves coming to understand oneself in relation to others; examining how society constructs privilege and inequality and how this affects one's own opportunities as well as those of different people; exploring the experiences of others and appreciating how those inform their worldviews, perspectives, and opportunities; and evaluating how schools and classrooms operate and can be structured to value diverse human experiences and to enable learning for all students (p. 201).

CHAPTER SUMMARY

The strength in the story of Ruby Bridges, her mother Lucille, and Barbara Henry is none of these three women imagined, when their paths crossed, they would become part of history. This journey began with Ruby's mother Lucille, who wanted her daughter to receive an excellent education. She sent Ruby to Frantz, unknowing the eyes of the country were on her daughter. Ruby's mother was doing what she thought was in the best interest of her child and within her sphere of influence, yet she had no idea of the impact her decision would have on her family and her community.

Ruby, not knowing anything about racism or integration, went to school every day and learned as much as she could from her teacher. Ruby did not understand until the end of her first year that the events in and around Frantz had transpired because she was black. Her actions within her sphere of influence impacted how the education of black children would forever be changed.

Barbara Henry just wanted to teach. She accepted a job in an integrated classroom based on her love of teaching. As Ruby's teacher, she did everything she could to protect Ruby as well as help her learn. Mrs. Henry believed every child was deserving of a quality education. She quickly learned her colleagues believed only white children could be educated. These incompatible ideas allowed Mrs. Henry to confront this dissonance. She continued to do what she loved; teach children. Equally important, she took action beyond her classroom and courageously confronted the building administrator who was perpetuating the inequity within the school.

How do the implications of this case study apply to teachers today? Across this country on a daily basis, teachers weigh decisions regarding what may be best for urban students. In doing so, they are influenced by an understanding of their students as well as realities, laws, and school policies that may be contrary to what they believe is best for their students. As they make their decisions, teachers must continually question assumptions and challenge perceptions in order to become effective educators in urban environments.

REFERENCES

Bridges, R. (1999). *Through my eyes: Articles and interviews compiled and edited by Margo Lundell.* New York: Scholastic Press.
Bridges, R., LLC. (2013). Ruby Bridges. Retrieved from www.rubybridges.com
Darling-Hammond, L. (2002). Education a profession for equitable practice. In L. Darling-Hammond., J. French, & S. P. Garcia-Lopez (Eds.), *Learning to teach for social justice* (pp. 201–212), New York: Teachers College Press.

Index

achievement gaps (A), 60–64. *See also* Value Line

action, 66–67; knowledge transforming into, 71–79; theory translated into, 81–86

activists, teachers as, 72–74

Aesop's Fable, 5

African Americans, 66, 81–86

analysis, autobiography, 8–9

appreciation, 45–48

apprehension, 45–48

aspirational capital, 49

autobiography: analysis, 8–9; communication, 7–9; cultural identity, 4–7; cultural understanding, 7–9; narrative, 7–8; overview of, 7–9

Ayers, William, 46

Bank Street College, 36–37

Bank Street School for Children, 28–30

best practices, 27

biases, 77

bill, 73

biography, 9

Bridges, Lucille, 82, 85

Bridges, Ruby, 81–86

Brown v. Board of Education, 64

Bureau of Educational Experiments, 36–37

California, 18, 20, 21

capital, 49–51

case study: Bank Street School for Children, 36, 37; Bridges, 81–86; cognitive dissonance, 81–86; poverty, 28–30, 36–37; social justice, 81–86; sphere of influence, 81–86

Census Bureau, U.S., 18, 22

cheating, 71

children: on free meals, 32; Jewish, 30–31; poverty influencing, 28–38; on reduced meals, 32; social context of, 27–38; in urban environments, 27–38; urban school, 46

About the Authors

Dr. Connie L. Schaffer earned her BS in secondary education from Kansas State University and her MS in special education and EdD in educational leadership and supervision from the University of Nebraska at Omaha (UNO). She is currently an assistant professor in the Teacher Education Department at UNO and the assessment coordinator for the UNO College of Education.

Prior to becoming a faculty member, Dr. Schaffer served as the coordinator for the Metropolitan Omaha Educational Consortium where she worked closely with the superintendents and other leaders of eleven school districts in the Omaha area. She also coordinated UNO's field experiences for seven years. In this role she collaborated with metro-Omaha schools to deliver field experiences, practicums, internships, and student teaching experiences as well as designed and implemented a pre-service Urban Immersion program in which teacher education courses were delivered within urban K–12 elementary and secondary schools.

As a faculty member, Dr. Schaffer and her students participate in urban Culture Walks each semester and spend approximately one-third of their course hours in urban schools. She has published several journal articles related to urban field experiences and has presented on this and other topics at international conferences. She is a member of Phi Delta Kappa, Kappa Delta Pi, Delta Kappa Gamma, the Horace Mann League, and the Association of Teacher Educators.

Connie can be contacted at cschaffer@unomaha.edu, via LinkedIn as Connie Schaffer, or on Twitter @ConnieCschaffer.

Dr. Meg White earned her BA in early childhood education from Marymount University, a MA in education, counseling and student services from San Jose State University, and an EdD in curriculum and teaching from Northcentral University.

Meg has been an educator for over thirty years. She spent fourteen years as a K–12 classroom teacher in public schools including Washington, D.C., and San Jose, California. From her teaching experiences came the passion to advocate for students and teachers in urban districts. When she made the transition to higher education, specifically working with pre-service teachers, she created programs to recruit and train pre-service teachers to be effective urban educators.

Meg began a school-supported fieldwork experience for pre-service teachers in Atlantic City, New Jersey. The intention of this fieldwork is to show pre-service teachers how the perceptions of urban schools and urban students may be different than the realities. Meg was selected as the 2015 Epicurean Society of Southern New Jersey Outstanding Educator Recognition Award recipient for her work with the Atlantic City schools. She has published and presented internationally on topics related to urban education.

Meg can be contacted via email at meg.white@stockton.edu, or via LinkedIn.

Dr. Corine (Cori) Cadle Meredith Brown earned her BS in elementary education from Bloomsburg University, a MEd in gifted education from University of Virginia, and a PhD in educational psychology from University of Virginia. A former elementary classroom teacher, she has worked in K–8 public schools in Pennsylvania, Virginia, New York, and New Jersey.

She currently serves as the assistant chair of the Interdisciplinary and Inclusive Education Department in the College of Education at Rowan University. Her research interests focus on learning communities, teaching and learning in urban environments, professional development school partnerships, and instructional strategies that encourage talent development in all learners. She also serves as the program coordinator for elementary education, teaching elementary methods at the undergraduate level and curriculum courses at the graduate level. At Rowan, Dr. Brown developed the Elementary Honors Clinical Practice, Honors Elementary Seminar, and Honors Teaching of Students with Linguistic and Cultural Differences cohort of courses.

Dr. Cori Meredith Brown is co-counselor of Rowan's Eta Psi chapter of Kappa Delta Pi, nationally recognized as a three-time ACE Award chapter by executive board members of the International Honor Society in Education. She has partnered as a Professor in Residence (PIR) at three elementary schools in New Jersey, and maintains active membership in the National Association of Professional Development Schools (NAPDS). Cori can be contacted via email at meredithc@rowan.edu, via LinkedIn as Cori Meredith Brown, or on Twitter @ProfessorCori.